THE SEED-PLANTING CHURCH

Nurturing Churches to Health

Changing Church Leaders from Maintenance Harvesters to Nurturing Seed-Planters, and Members from Donors to Disciples

WALDO J. WERNING

ChurchSmart
RESOURCES

St. Charles, IL 60174
1-800-253-4276

ChurchSmart
RESOURCES

Published by ChurchSmart Resources

We are an evangelical Christian publisher committed to producing excellent products at affordable prices to help church leaders accomplish effective ministry in the areas of Church planting, Church growth, Church renewal and Leadership development.

For a free catalog of our resources call 1-800-253-4276.

Cover design by: Julie Becker

© copyright 2003
by Waldo J. Werning

ISBN: 1-889638-36-6

THE SEED-PLANTING CHURCH

BIOGRAPHIC INFORMATION

Dr. Waldo J. Werning served congregations in Missouri and Oklahoma. For 50 years he has been a stewardship/biblical renewal executive and counselor for districts and congregations in the United States, and in 16 other countries. He served as chairman/secretary for his denominational mission board for 10 years, and chairman for Lutheran Bible Translators for 20 years. He was a participant in the Lausanne Congress of World Evangelism and a sectional speaker at the Manila Congress. Author of 30 books, Dr. Werning is the Director of the Discipleship/Stewardship Center of Pewaukee, Wisconsin and retired from Concordia Theological Seminar. Originator of the *Empowering and Mobilizing God's People* discipling series and stewardship series, his most recent books are *12 Pillars of a Healthy Church* and *God Says Move—Go Where He Leads*.

RECOGNITION AND APPRECIATION

To Ruth, my seed-planting, nurturing, loving spouse of 58 years. Ruth's nurturing ministry as a pastor's wife, mother, grandmother, great-grandmother, master teacher, mentor to learning-disabled and gifted children, Stephen Minister, inspirational speaker and leader, and choir member to the praise of God—all motivated by the Gospel of Jesus Christ to help develop and disciple many in God's field to be what God calls them to be to the glory of Jesus. Spiritual enabler to me, Ruth has helped me keep my mind and heart on Jesus!

To Sharon Jones (MM, MA), my daughter, for her kind and helpful assistance in editing the manuscript.

To hundreds of gifted church leaders who shared generously with me through all these years the grace and knowledge of Seed-planting ministries they received from the Lord, and the many pastors, laymen and laywomen who enriched my life and ministry with their insights which God provided by the variety of gifts in the body of Christ.

To the Triune God whose abundant grace and Spirit directed my ministry of writing to plant these seeds for encouraging God's seed-planters to tend to all of the precious souls in God's field.

Dr. Waldo J. Werning
April 16, 2003

ABOUT THE BIBLE TRANSLATION USED IN THIS BOOK AND THE MISSION SOCIETY THAT PRODUCED IT...

WHAT kind of translation is *GOD'S WORD*®? *Answer:* It's the Bible for the neXt generation… and the next… and the next! It's the one to use to reach young people with "THE truth that will set them free" (John 8:32)! These young men and women, teenagers, and children have hopes, dreams, and needs. But their greatest need is to have a relationship with Jesus—to grasp the importance of what he has done for them… and what he wants to do in and through them! And that will happen only as the Holy Spirit has opportunity to work in their lives through God's life-changing word!

And WHY is *GOD'S WORD*® the translation to use? WHY is it the best "seed" to use to reach the neXt generation… and the next… and the next? *Answer:*

- ◆ *GOD'S WORD* is FAITHFUL to the original meaning of the Hebrew, Aramaic, and Greek languages through which God spoke to his people in earlier days.

- ◆ And, *GOD'S WORD* communicates God's life-changing message of salvation in clear, natural English to all his people today—*churched* and (especially) *unchurched*, *educated* and *less-educated*, *older* and (especially) *younger*. Its single-column, open layout makes it especially easy to read and understand. In fact, *GOD'S WORD* is the MOST READABLE (2nd grade to scholar) English translation available (apart from a few "simplified" versions)!

- ◆ In addition, *GOD'S WORD* incorporates nearly perfect English GRAMMAR! In other words, you can teach English from the text!

WHAT kind of organization is God's Word to the Nations? *Answer:* We're a mission society—a mission resource for God's people in mission! Our mission society managed and funded the translation of *GOD'S WORD*®.

OUR VISION

To be used by the Holy Spirit to promote and support the biblical outreach strategy—"BECOME A SEED PLANTER AND CHANGE LIVES"—among God's people so that they may become active participants in his mission *"to seek and to save people who are lost"* (Luke 19:19)!

FOR MORE INFORMATION

Visit us at *www.godsword.org* —or— call us toll free at 1-877-GOD'S WORD.

TABLE OF CONTENTS

Foreword...13

Introduction..15

Chapter One
A Satellite View of Productive Agriculture............................21

Chapter Two
A Satellite Divine View of the Traditional "Harvesting" Church..........27

Chapter Three
God Expects His Church to Plant Seeds and Nurture His Fields 35

Chapter Four
The Dimensions and Goals of a Seed-Planting, Nurturing Church 51

Chapter Five
Abundant Stewardship Harvests Come from Abundant Planting
and Nurturing...65

Chapter Six
The Seed-Planting, Nurturing Church Cares for the Entire Field 101

Chapter Seven
Healthy Churches Use Quality Control Systems 125

Chapter Eight
Leaders with Faith that Produces Character and a Heart Like God ...141

Chapter Nine
If you Want Spiritual Fruit, You Have to Get Out of the Cathedral-Barn . 151

Appendix A..157

Endnotes 165

Commendations 169

FOREWORD

By Dr. Robert E. Logan

Waldo Werning reminds me of a modern day Caleb because he's always learning and always growing. Now over 80 years old, he is still active in kingdom work, eager to see God's word go forth and be embraced. One of the qualities I want to have, as long as I have life and breath, is to continue to grow and learn and make whatever contribution I can to the advance of God's kingdom. In that sense, Waldo Werning is a role model for me.

As one who has always had a focus on the harvest, I recognize the importance of laying the strong groundwork necessary to see that future harvest become a reality. Werning challenges us to look at the processes that need to be cultivated and implemented in order to reap a bountiful harvest. He looks at church health and growth from a holistic systems approach, recognizing how all the various facets of church life contribute to producing a unified whole—a church that wholeheartedly lives out its mission.

Churches that take Werning's principles to heart and strategically focus on planting, watering, and fertilizing will find the harvest growing proportionally larger as they shift their focus outward—for the work of farming and harvesting is done out in the fields, not in the barn. God calls us to look beyond programs and ecclesiastical structures. Instead, we are called to become a community of faith who live in close relationship with the living God, capable of reaching the mission fields all around us.

The **Seed-Planting Church** is in many ways a groundbreaking book to help leaders think differently about church and how they carry out its ministries to accomplish God's intended result. You'll find the book thoroughly biblical, filled with practical insights, and deeply challenging. I'd encourage you to read carefully, to reflect and pray, asking God for the next steps toward implementing these principles in your own ministry context.

INTRODUCTION

The Seed-Planting Church

Imagine a farmer out cleaning the edges of his deep green, lush, flourishing field of corn, seeing that every acre and every plant is growing toward maturity with full ears of corn. Then imagine another farmer sitting in his barn, frantic and desperate, discussing with a helper how he can maintain and survive his acreage with only 40% strong and healthy, while 60% is blighted and shriveled and barely alive.

Now as you concentrate on Jesus' and Paul's agricultural analogies and pictures of the church, answer the question about which farmer represents most closely most of the traditional churches of our day?

The Seed-Planting Church reveals and unveils the failure of 80% of churches to recognize and change their dysfunctional condition which the scriptures show to be unacceptable. The first two chapters of my book introduce this relevant and urgent matter which has dire consequences if not changed. It is a miracle of God's grace that maintenance churches can survive with most of their members passive and not functioning according to their creation and calling in Christ.

You will see that the assumption or postulate of my book is that God intended to build seed-planting, nurturing, mission churches, not institutional, organizational, maintenance, harvesting churches. This in no way belittles or is negative about "harvest theology" or "harvest evangelism," for the problem lies with a "harvest practice or strategy," which embodies and depends upon maintenance and technocratic strategies without seed-planting and nurturing as its basic focus.

Is this seed-planting, nurturing redesign of church strategy achieved in the book? A number of evangelical mission leaders in America attest that it does. The "Church Doctor" writes, "Powerfully practical…will change your church from a bureaucracy to the movement that God has called Christianity to be…I have already begun to use this material with churches." A denominational Director for North American Missions asserts, "The author has put his finger on the basic issue of the church in North America. Will it be an institution or will it be part of the missional movement?" The respected Dean of the School of Religion at a Christian University commends that the author "has seen a neglected niche in church planting and has written a well-crafted book to meet the need." The Director of the Center for U.S. Missions at another Christian University writes, "A trip to an Iowa farm and a review of the Biblical agriculture narratives provide the author with a powerful metaphor to help us distinguish the problem facing today's churches." A Seminary Mission Professor who has written many books tells, "The author proposes a radical redesign of church strategy based on Biblical principles and examples."

By God's grace I have been privileged to be a servant of Christ in His Kingdom for many years, visiting over 1000 churches, and discipling pastors and church leaders of churches in 16 countries. A church leader who has studied God's Word while observing the condition and the functioning of churches would be blind or at least have myopia not to observe what is reported in these pages.

What do church observers and analysts say about churches today? Recently, Tim Stafford of *Christianity Today* reported frustration as he interviewed George Barna.[1] According to Stafford, Barna tells of having kept a fierce pace over the past six years, spending more than half his time away from home. Barna said, "I didn't want to admit that what I thought might work had failed." His aim was to lead church leaders into revitalizing the church. "The strategy was flawed because it had an assumption," Barna went on. "The assumption was that the people in leadership are actually leaders. I thought all I need to do is give them the right information and they can draw the right conclusions."

At Willow Creek, Barna had experienced "the difference that a clear articulated vision could make, but most church leaders only seemed to grasp for a program that 'worked.'" He believed that "nothing's changing, and the change that we see is not for the better." Stafford observes, "In the long run, he hopes to cultivate a new generation of leaders, locating them as early as high school and challenging them to participate in strategic development of their capacities to lead for Christ. Twenty or thirty years from now, he hopes to see the result in a healthy, dynamic church."

Barna adds some challenges for American churches and Christianity, such as: "None of the same won't get any farther down the road of genuine discipleship.... Every day the church is becoming more like the world it allegedly seeks to change. At what point does that collapse become a 'crisis' and merit concentrated and strategic response? ... People pick and choose the Bible content they like or feel comfortable with but ignore the rest of God's counsel.... A costless faith - Christianity has no cost in America."

Barna believes the problem is in leadership. He says, "They do not have or understand vision. They are incapable of motivating and mobilizing people around God's vision. They fail to direct people's energies and resources effectively and efficiently."[2]

The Seed-Planting Church proposes an additional view. Yes, leadership problems must be addressed carefully, beginning with a focus on character and a godly heart, not depending on skill training. The basic issue is one of having the wrong strategic design. The design is often that of a programmatic, maintenance, harvesting church instead of a missional, seed-planting, nurturing church. This institutional church in its traditional design tries to renew itself with leaders who mold the church in programmatic or organizational ways. But the church will not be revitalized outside God's design.

God's design is a biblical model. It is the organic, natural body of Christ. It becomes a "community of faith" church. It is led by ordinary gifted leaders who adopt a *missional seed-planting* model in the place of a *maintenance harvesting* style of the church.

The institutional and organizational Christianity, established by Constantine 1700 years ago, has handicapped the church. It has demanded too high a cost. Luther's biblical emphasis on the priesthood of all believers changed the church landscape drastically. There were so many traditional and cultural barriers, however, that the biblical redesign of the church has never been completed.

When the Christian church came to America, it was independent of the State. It was completely free to introduce biblical practices. Programmatic innovations were introduced while some European habits and traditions were dropped. American Protestant churches developed their own forms and traditions. Renewal and revitalization of organizational, traditional churches came as a result of evangelical creativity. About 80 percent of American churches today are hampered by being basically harvesting models that depend on bigger and better programs, projects, budgets and institutional achievements.

Today, about 20 percent of all American Protestant churches possess most of the ingredients of the nurturing New Testament church. However, while the specific components of these vibrant, biblical churches are present, few have been structurally redesigned or have included or assimilated all the necessary renewal ingredients. Some of the influences of the maintenance harvesting church are still present. Few are an organic, natural body of Christ, a community of faith, a nurturing church, without some institutional and programmatic components and activities that are a drag on the church.

The traditional, programmatic, harvesting formula for church practice is flawed. **The Seed-Planting Church** exposes the weaknesses and failures of the institutional, harvesting church, while it presents the Scriptural basis and a fresh explanation of how we can design today's church as a seed-planting, fertilizing, and watering church. Accomplishing this goal requires more than highly skilled, trained visionary leaders and more than a high-powered program with various elements to put into place.

Renewal will never happen by the ordinary practice of the many traditional churches which remold the forms and activities by some new program from time to time. This book proposes a redesign of church strategy based on biblical principles and examples – a new and different design than the church of the last 17 centuries. Call it the Apostolic Church or whatever you wish to name it; the design grows clearly out of biblical texts to be freed from all institutional and programmatic constraints.

The seed-planting, nurturing church will be a creation of God by the Holy Spirit through men and women of faith. This community of faith is made up of leaders who embody and live in close relationship and communion with the living God in Jesus Christ, who multiply themselves by the Holy Spirit through the Word in the body of Christ.

The more than 20 percent of effective, growing churches which have visionary leaders with strong faith will eagerly make certain that all the biblical components and modules are in place, and will recognize themselves as a seed-planting rather than a harvesting church. The 80 percent of churches that are struggling in a maintenance or even in a survival mode, having plateaued or stagnated, find it difficult to gain adequately equipped and mobile leaders and members. The success of the church is not dependent upon what we can bring to a harvesting church, but what God gives to us in the seed-planting, nurturing church.

INTRODUCTION

Summarizing, the 80 percent of churches that are traditional, harvesting churches have a primary ministry to members, usually one entry point – Sunday morning worship. They repeat basically the same programs and activities and focus on traditional programs, treating symptoms while going from crisis to crisis. The 20 percent create multiple entry points for people to be involved, seek creative ways to nurture relationships, focus on outreach, minister to the hurts and hopes of people, and experience growth in ministry and mission. Harvesting churches exist with traditional rituals, legalisms and maintenance routines with considerable individualism and disconnected members, while seed-planting churches are grace-based with people connected and related to each other in ministry. The first is churchianity oriented and the second is Christianity oriented.

The future belongs to men and women of deep faith. It belongs to the Joshuas who fight battles like Jericho, and the Davids facing giants like Goliath. It does not belong to those who believe they can accomplish God's work through unique strategies and programs. It belongs to men and women who recognize their weaknesses. It belongs to those who have nothing to bring but a great big faith in a great big God. After all, the success of the church is only what *God* gives when the seed is planted and nurtured.

My hope is that by the time you finish this book, you will have a greater awareness of God's resources, of His incredible power, and of the ways in which He desires to extend His blessing on the church of today. It is also my hope that this book will encourage you to avoid using methods and technology to solve spiritual problems. I hope to share insights that will guide you to God's all-powerful Word instead of spending time on man-made solutions.

My ultimate goal is to help you see that this "agricultural project" of the church in which we are God's partners, is first and foremost the Lord's field, not ours. The vision is worthy and workable, for it comes from God and His Word. Only when we see this will we be able to grow healthy, nurturing churches. So let's get started. It's time to survey the fields, seeds, plants, fertilizer, and necessary water in the seed-planting nurturing, missional church. It is this church in which we are God's coworkers and managers – God's "farmers," if you will. This is His spiritual enterprise in which He alone gives the increase. To Him be the glory.

Waldo J. Werning

CHAPTER 1

A Satellite View of Productive Agriculture

As an Iowa farm youth 60 years ago, typical corn yield was around 50-60 bushels to the acre with the help of some fertilizer. A whole new world in agriculture was opened to me in the summer of 2002—the Global Positioning System. Visiting the Iowa farm of my niece and her husband, I learned about a precision system that, with the aid of a computer and software, maximizes crop potentials.

SATELLITE PRECISION MAXIMIZES CROP PRODUCTIVITY

Looking at a satellite view of the farm on the computer screen, I was shown the yield map of the corn harvest of a 142-acre field that averaged 190 bushels per acre. A click on the computer to one specific area showed the lowest yield of 140 bushels, while a click on another area showed that 245 bushels was the highest.

There was more to learn. The satellite map revealed the strengths and weaknesses of the soil in each portion of the field. Jim had done sample testing for nutrient minerals throughout the field. On the basis of that testing, satellite positioning showed the specific strengths and deficiencies of each particular section. Another satellite image revealed the chemical spraying operation which helped increase crop yield productivity by eliminating destructive weeds and insects.

Jim then showed me the chip that is inserted into the computer on his tractor. This chip has a prescription for precise placement of what food is needed in the soil. A fertilizing implement meters the requirements of each specific area of the ground. The computer chip, the tractor's "brain," controls what the fertilizer spreader, planter, or sprayer applies. It enables the farmer to skillfully administer seed, fertilizer, or chemicals appropriate for each acre. The result? Vital soil nutrients and food needed by the seeds for maximum growth and fruitfulness are supplied.

Jim tells that the Global Positioning System (GPS) guides him throughout every step of the process. This guidance comes from what is called a "light bar." "I test for nutrients at each specific site," he says. "On the basis of those results, the light bar on the tractor guides me to feed the soil precisely what it needs, or to spray the correct applications in order to thwart weeds and insects. I track yield on every inch of ground and use satellite imaging to continually monitor the crops throughout the process." This is how every acre with every plant is nurtured and monitored for maximum care and productivity.

Because of soil type and fertility differences, some plants need more food and some less. The ground needs a proper balance of fertilizers – nitrogen, phosphorous and potash. Lime helps to neutralize soil acidity. Zinc and sulfur may be needed at times for balance. Some plants may need certain additional nutrients due to specific soil deficiencies. This type of individualized application is a nutritionally sound way to maximize cropland potential. For accurate evaluation, infrared technology assesses and details the health of the crop.

The global positioning and guidance system is an almost "supernatural" aid. With GPS, tractors are less like a machine and more like a moving computer. It allows the farmer to care for his acreage in a way that would be humanly impossible, if it were left to his own resources. The unique system unlocks the potential of huge tracts of land, of farms spreading across hundreds of acres. All summed up, it helps farmers have the most efficient production possible. All of this is accomplished without even mentioning agronomic services, superior crop genetics, water management and irrigation systems, and the elimination of pollution. Using an old idiom, the sky is the limit.

EVERY ACRE AND PLANT IS CULTIVATED, TENDED, AND NURTURED

Farmers and agricultural workers will not survive in their business unless every acre is carefully cultivated, nurtured, and managed. A successful farmer does everything possible in order to have healthy plants, vines, and branches. Every possible means of maximizing cropland potential is on his mind every day. Cultivation, nurture, food, protection, management of every resource on every acre and every plant he owns is his aim. No matter the effort, the goal is a healthy crop. If he does anything less, he will fail in his enterprise. That is the reason agriculturists today use modern technology and science. That is the reason they employ a global guidance system. That is the reason they pay attention to every detail, making certain their entire farm, vineyard or orchard is carefully watched from above.

Christian farmers and agriculturists recognize that weather and amounts of rain cannot be controlled by technology where irrigation is not available. After planting and cultivating, Christians recognize that crops are entirely in God's hand, and that they have done as much as they can with their talents and time. At this time, they place complete faith and trust in God for timely rain to produce the crop – and for the blessing of weather that will not damage it.

A SEED-PLANTING, NURTURING, NOT HARVESTING MINDSET

The flourishing farmer has a seed-planting, fertilizing, watering, feeding, and caring mindset, not one of sitting around waiting for the harvest in order to enjoy the reward of selling a crop. He does not have a harvest mindset that focuses on the most profitable acres, while ignoring those acres with plants and fruit trees which are less productive, because he does not have the time to tend all of them or he does not need the money from the least of them.

After the harvest, when he looks at the computer yield map, the nurturing farmer will not decide to ignore or dismiss 20 percent of the acreage and plants and fruit trees because they are less productive. Rather, he studies carefully how to increase production by gaining better genetics, providing stronger nutrients, applying chemicals and spraying more widely. This assures that even the lesser crops will be more fruitful.

No prosperous agriculturist has a harvest mindset. He has a seed-planting, fertilizing, and watering mindset. As he tends and manages his acreage carefully and faithfully, his mind is on quality and quantity. His yield map reveals the amount of attention he has given to his land and his produce, rather than merely sitting idly by while hoping for a large harvest.

JESUS HAS HIS EYES ON THE FIELDS, TOO

Agriculture is closely related to Jesus' teaching and ministry from the physical and spiritual viewpoints. Food, wheat, grapes, and figs are familiar topics integrally connected to His messages. Jesus taught that God's Word is the seed (Luke 8:11-15). The Holy Spirit enables His people to plant, fertilize, and water that seed in order to produce bountiful fruit. His parables reveal that He fully expected healthy plants to grow and be nurtured to productivity.

The Bible is full of agricultural and food imagery that richly intermingles with both physical and spiritual applications of plants, vines, and trees. 2 Corinthians 9:10 makes it clear: "God gives seed to the farmer and food to those who need to eat. God will also give you seed and multiply it. In your lives He will increase the things you do that have His approval."

Paul refers to "spiritual seed" that has been planted (1 Corinthians 9:11). In teaching how the dead will come back to life on the final day, Paul says, "The seed you plant doesn't come to life unless it dies first. What you plant, whether it's wheat or something else, is only a seed. It doesn't have the form that the plant will have. God gives the plant the form he wants it to have. Each kind of seed grows into its own form.... When the body is planted, it decays. When it comes back to life, it cannot decay. When the body is planted, it doesn't have any splendor and is weak. When it comes back to life, it has splendor and is strong. It is planted as a physical body. It comes back to life as a spiritual body. As there is a physical body, so there is also a spiritual body" (1 Corinthians 15:36-38, 42-44). This teaching ends with the great shout, "Thank God that he gives us the victory through our Lord Jesus Christ" (1 Corinthians 15:57).

Jesus wanted His people to richly share in His provision and abundance. He made this clear in both the earthly and heavenly spheres. He wanted believers to know their priorities in seeking heavenly food. In John 4: 31-34 we read, "The disciples were urging him, 'Rabbi, have something to eat.' Jesus told them, 'I have food to eat that you don't know about.' The disciples asked each other, 'Did someone bring Him something to eat?' Jesus told them, 'My food is to do what the One who sent me wants me to do and to finish the work He has given me.'" His every breath, His very sustenance in life, was doing the work God had given Him to do.

The scriptures show Jesus to be spiritual food, and the Word to be the seed. We read, "You have been born again, not from a seed that can be destroyed, but through God's everlasting word that can't be destroyed" (1 Peter 1:23). Isaiah 61:11 tells how the Word as Seed brings forth fruit, "Like the ground that brings forth its crops and like a garden that makes the seed in it grow, so the Almighty Lord will make righteousness and praise spring up in front of all nations."

NURTURING VINES AND TREES FOR PRODUCTIVITY

In John 15: 1-9, Jesus teaches that He is the Vine and we are the branches. Living in Him, disciples will produce much fruit. Without Him there will be no harvest. Also, production of fruit is a sign of true discipleship. Jesus tells His disciples that the Father "removes every one of my branches that doesn't produce fruit. He also prunes every branch that does produce fruit to make it produce more fruit." In fact, whoever does not live in Him is "thrown away like a branch and dries up. Branches like this are gathered, thrown in to a fire, and burned." Such non-productivity is a tragedy. When the branch is connected to the Vine, the branch pictures a disciple productively connected to Christ. Fruit-bearing branches of vines and trees are God's requirement in the kingdom of Christ and of the Church. Jesus concludes, "You give glory to my Father when you produce a lot of fruit."

One day as Jesus was on His way to Jerusalem, He was hungry. Seeing a fig tree by the road, He went up to the tree but found nothing but leaves. He said to it, "May fruit never grow on you again!" (Matthew 21:18-19). The tree was worthless because it produced nothing.

THE GPS AND THE DPS

Jesus' action about a fruitless tree seems harsh and possibly even cruel. It isn't! The reason why is that Jesus who with the Father created the world, made everything for a purpose. Likewise, He saved us for a purpose—to bear fruit and to bear it abundantly (John 10:10). "God has made us what we are. He has created us in Christ Jesus to live lives filled with good works that he has prepared for us to do." (Ephesians 2:10).

Like the technology the GPS has given the farmer, industries, transportation and governments needing information and direction, God has given Christians and the Church the DPS (Divine Positioning System). However, the DPS is not in the sky to read what is happening on earth, but it is a gift of God which is the means for our reading by which we know what God has to say about church and what we can learn about His will and way.

Some Christians are influenced for their behavior and life by WWJD ("What Would Jesus Do?") Some even wear the bracelet or pin. But it goes much farther than asking that question! Fundamentally, church leaders who want to build a healthy church must ask, "What Did Jesus **Say**? (WDJS).

WDJS is such a basic issue that we might be reminded of Vince Lombardi beginning a lecture to football professionals while holding up a ball and saying, "This is a football!" For church leaders and professionals, is it too obvious that we should not hold up a specific book and say, "This is a B-I-B-L-E?" That Bible is our Divine Positioning System! That DPS gives church leaders the principles and components to change a traditional church to a healthy church.

When a veteran national church growth/healthy church author views this book as "thinking outside **the box**," obviously his reference is to think beyond traditional church models. This book looks directly to the Word of God as the Box! It challenges you **to think in the Box—the Word**. Throughout these pages, the consistent challenge is WDJS.

More than that—this book supplies you with more of the DPS by adding WDPS ("What Did **Paul** Say?"). Paul also expounded on farmer and agrarian language and concepts to teach us the truths of the components of a seed-planting, nurturing church.

So, it's time to move on to a satellite (divine) view of the traditional church—and WDJS and WDPS. Then we will walk up and down the Biblical paths of Jesus' and Paul's teachings to review the divine impact of the Word (thinking in THE Box!) to recognize the DPS for planting seeds and nurturing God's field for healthy Christians and Churches.

CHAPTER 2

A Satellite Divine View of the Traditional "Harvesting" Church

How often has our church vision been clouded and blinded by foggy lenses? When we look through "institutional" lenses of our church experiences, we do not see what God sees. Human and pragmatic considerations of maintenance and harvesting often blind us. We actually cheat ourselves. The fact is, God sees much more than we do.

What does God see? On one hand, He sees churches proclaiming the saving Gospel of Jesus Christ. He sees believers committed to the call of ministering to people at their point of need. He sees equipping churches that consistently plant and water. He sees churches that cultivate and fertilize to enjoy a good harvest.

On the other hand, God sees institutional churches, ones often marked by their imposing structure and traditions. The "ecclesiastical satellite" sees churches striving to maintain members, workers, and programs. The heavenly view sees the body of Christ struggling to produce a harvest from fields that have too often been neglected.

A PARABLE OF A HARVESTER AND HIS ORCHARD

The traditional harvesting church is like a farmer and his four hundred fruit trees. In the middle of the orchard is a cathedral-barn filled with enough nutrients to nurture the trees. From the divine satellite the 400 trees represent 400 members of a traditional, institutional, harvesting church. The farmer and his helpers have a harvesting mentality and outlook. What the satellite sees is 400 fruit trees of which 200 are regular producers, 100 are slight producers, and 100 are non-producers.

The farmer with the harvesting mindset has weekly contact with the productive trees. They visit the nurturing barn each Sunday to be watered, nourished, and encouraged to bear much fruit. Despite personal encouragement to gather more frequently, many less productive trees come only periodically. They seem to have little concern for nutrition. The non-productive trees simply never come. Once a year, more or less, the farmer sends a farm-worker to the unfruitful trees and reminds them that they should be coming to the barn for their nutrition.

The weekly gathering at the cathedral-barn provides beneficial encouragement. Messages and songs focus the trees' hearts on the temporary nature of this earthly farm and that the Lord of the universe will one day take them to the eternal garden. The farmer and workers, however, find it necessary to remind the trees regularly that fertilizer here on earth is costly. In order for nutrition to be available through the year, the trees will need to contribute to continual maintenance costs.

The harvesting mentality is a long-standing tradition in which the trees find purpose in the fruit that they provide for the farmer. It is a tradition in which the farmer is basically a harvester, not one whose focus is to leave the cathedral-barn to plant seeds, cultivate, fertilize and water the fields and the trees.

THE HARVESTING CHURCH CONTRASTED WITH THE SEED-PLANTING, NURTURING CHURCH

The parable of the fruit trees shows us in stark terms what the "Divine Satellite" might observe in a harvest-minded church. The organizationally structured church is often focused on rituals and traditions it believes must be kept. It is geared to religious regulations and often views periodic attendance at worship as a means of being a good church member or even "staying in favor with God." Though never stated as such, knowledge is expected more in such a church than is living faith. Even though it may not be recognized, the emphasis is very much on external deeds that God "rewards." Certain procedures or ways of doing things are considered "right" while others may be considered "wrong."

In contrast, the church focused on cultivating and nurturing offers a type of spirituality that involves relationships—a living relationship with God and with His people. This church is constantly growing not only in grace, but in knowledge and faith. The cultivating mindset results in true worship of the Almighty living God, active service toward God and people, and accountability to each other in the body of Christ. All of this is a natural response to God's love as shown in Christ Jesus.

The harvest-minded church has little transparency. Relationships center around duties to be performed. The pastor and members concern themselves with questions like, "What needs to be done in order to maintain this institution? What can we do to assure it will survive? How can we fill pews and how will bills be paid?" Intimacy is rare.

On the other hand, the church focused on cultivation is geared to the Great Commission and mission outreach. It asks, "What is our purpose here at this time? What is God's call and assignment for us?" The will of God is actively sought in all matters. The concern is not for what the **institution** wants, but rather what **God** desires. Its primary commitment is the increase of the kingdom of God, making disciples of those who are a part of the body. It fosters a living Christian community. Relationships thrive.

The church set basically on harvesting has managerial tendencies. It is sometimes paralyzed by an institutionalism that accentuates structures, control, and various types of legalistic demands. These practices are usually born of long-standing traditions. Set ways of doing things "drive" people and tend to become the core of church life. Quite frankly, the prescribed procedures hamper the possibility of encountering God.

In contrast, the seed-planting, nurturing church sets members free to do God's work. It does not see the pastor as the only leader. It grows as God directs and is not limited to structures or traditional programs. The pastor sees all of Christ's body working together, from the least to the greatest, from the "invisible" parts to the very visible ones. Believing scripture, he knows that Christ has sufficiently supplied all the workers with spiritual gifts needed in His church. He believes Jesus continues to do so as new ministries arise. Members become increasingly aware of what **God** has done, that He is doing things in a new way and a bigger way than they have seen before.

Harvesting and institutionalism are present when people want to be served, more than to serve. It is seen when obedience to church practices is emphasized to the neglect of Biblical sanctification and the spiritual quality of life. The harvesting mode is to invite people to exult Christ but then allow them to accept comfortable church membership, cultural morality, and salvation by performing the right rituals.

The church focused on nurturing, however, provides spiritual food to strengthen them for service and ministry. The church's purposes are recognized as being the very purposes of God. His purposes are kept at the center of everything the corporate body says and does. They understand the concept of sanctification; that what each Christian says and does in the body flows out of the grace given by Christ's sacrifice for them on the cross.

The institutional church is focused considerably on forms and technologies. Its eyes are on statistics and its concerns are about plans, programs and budgets. New programs and by-laws often seem to give great hope for the future. "Cosmetic" approaches touch up forms and methods that supposedly will add new life to the church. But in reality, ministry and mission are still bound by institutional restrictions.

By contrast, the seed-planting nurturing church has the distinguishing mark of seeking the Holy Spirit's leading for more effective ministry. It models the mission of the church by Scriptural principles. The powerful Word of God enables it to engage in new and growing ministries. This kind of cultivating church creatively changes forms and functions in a way that allows God's grace to be expressed without human restrictions.

The maintenance harvesting church finds itself immobilized by a variety of obstacles. Many individual members may actually be "paralyzed" by television, "spectatoritis," or any number of activities that are unproductive for our purpose in life. They may find themselves enslaved by bondage to habits and sins or emotional frames of mind. Hours, weeks, months, and even years of Christians' lives may be wasted. Committees and boards often become disabled by lack of focus. Little more happens than fruitless discussion and disagreements. Programs achieve little more than maintaining the church.

The nurturing church, on the other hand, is not restrained by cultural barriers or church structures. Members are not paralyzed into inaction, but rather are motivated to do the work of Christ in the world around them. Excitement about the mission of the church abounds. The people are mobilized to go, to teach and to baptize. They edify each other, preparing God's people for works of service, in order to build up the body of Christ (Ephesians 4:12). They witness of Jesus Christ by the power of the Holy Spirit. As a result, the seed-planting nurturing church's home base is the launching pad into its community and the entire world.

The maintenance-oriented church is overly concerned with harvesting fruit. It "shakes trees" in order to reap finances and workers. Fruit pickers are critically dependent upon these workers and dollars in order to survive. Out of sheer survival instinct, a pressure cooker attitude causes them to panic at the thought of not meeting goals and budgets. "How will the church fill positions?" they ask. "How can we complete tasks so that the work gets done? How will it all be financed?" The church becomes emotionally and physically controlled by urgent demands of human goals for fruit. Even worse is the fact that these needs are proclaimed through programs that are often equated as being God's will.

The cultivating church, however, concentrates on the roots of the plants and the pruning, just like Jesus did. That church holds itself responsible, by the power of the Spirit, to cultivate, nourish, and water the ground. After all, there can be no healthy or abundant fruit without nourished roots. Members understand their call to nourish and be nourished and that God promises to provide the increase.

Our Lord told of the owner who asked his gardener to cut down the tree that had been unproductive. The gardener pleaded for the owner to allow him to dig around the tree and fertilize it for one more year. He wanted to give it a chance to become a healthy tree, filled with fruit (Luke 13:6-9). Leaders of nurturing churches are caretakers who plead with God to give them time to cultivate. They nourish the members of the church so that they might bear abundant fruit. Such gardeners use a process of biblical discipleship that grows healthy trees before expecting fruit.

The harvesting church has a microwave mentality by which a button is to be pushed so that soon a successful program is produced. This places pressure on leaders to contrive successful programs rather than conducting an educational process with biblical goals which effectively penetrates minds and hearts. They actually find themselves having to force a superficial or structured sort of Christianity, one that produces results in an artificial way. The result sometimes is that the church is soliciting "cut-flower" commitments for the tasks at hand.

This is not true of the nurturing church. Its members have been fed by God's Word in a way that effectively penetrates their minds and hearts. Leaders commit themselves to Scriptural principles throughout the entire course of growth. They look for spiritual results, from seed-time to harvest. These leaders develop a systematic educational process for growing fully devoted disciples of Jesus Christ. Members are involved in Bible study ranging from the very basic ones to the challenging—all of it profitable for meaningful life change (2 Timothy 3:16-17).

The harvesting church emphasizes being good church members. But what is a good or bad church member? This kind of church membership centers on activities to the detriment of spiritual growth with the result that members are satisfied to belong to the "church" without acquiring maturity. The nurturing church places the accent on Christians who grow and mature through study of the Word.

The harvesting church thinks in terms of converts and donors, emphasizing membership and the duties of church members. The nurturing church sees every member as a disciple of Christ, recognizing that conversion is but a first step to be followed by a lifetime of Christian growth, maturity and discipleship. Christian nurture and education are offered as the central part of all of life through small groups meeting for interactive Bible studies and support for specific needs. Only disciple making will assure care of all believers and lead to world evangelization.

The vital signs of a congregation are not the numbers and the dollars, but the changed lives of those who have become active disciples by the teaching of the Word. Maturing the saints is the congregation's mission, and it occurs only through the Word.

Maintenance, harvesting churches have in reality replaced the Word with programs and other creative ways of trying to maintain the church. The problem with their members is that they are not where instruction in the Word is happening. The seed stays in the bin.

The seed-planting nurturing church knows as the old Broadway song reminds us that "A song is not a song until you sing it. A bell is not a bell until you ring it." A seed is no good until you plant it. The Word in a person's life is not effective until it is proclaimed and taught. The nurturing church sings the song, rings the bell, plants the seed, and makes certain that the people are where instruction in the Word happens.

God's grace raises the church beyond the mediocrity of programmatic, harvesting methodologies to be a seed-planting, nurturing, missional church.

The question remains: "What does the divine satellite see in our church?"

A VIVID PICTURE

As we conclude listing the contrasts between the seed-planting, nurturing church and the programmatic, maintenance harvesting church, will you envision a mental picture of a vivid green, leafy, dense plant and then visualize another plant with lonely stems with shriveled, brown, dry leaves. This is the general spiritual condition of members of traditional churches, which usually have less than 40% who are lively and active in some way, while about 60% are marginal and inactive. An owner of such a plant would not tolerate it. How long will leaders of traditional churches condone, permit and accept such a situation with dysfunctional members? **The Seed-Planting Church** seeks to provide the biblical answer.

CHAPTER 3

God Expects His Church to Plant Seeds and Nurture His Field

As God's eyes scan the whole world (2 Chronicles 16:9a)—its billions of people, its sprawling cities—He gazes deeply into the manner in which His Church ministers the saving and sanctifying Word. Whether it is a church of fifty, two hundred, six hundred, or four thousand members, the Church is where He offers His Word as Seed. His desire is for that Seed to grow. God desires that His people be productive.

Just as a satellite map helps to accurately assess the productivity of an Iowa cornfield, the parable of the farmer and the fruit farm helps to assess productivity in the church. It prompts Christians and churches to take a look at the Word of God and see it as the seed, fertilizer, and water needed to produce fruit. The almighty Word itself is what nourishes spiritual plants in the kingdom of Christ and His Church.

That Word is the seed that brings growth to the people of God. Jesus told His disciples the story of a farmer who went to plant seeds (Luke 8:4-15). "Some seeds were planted along the road, were trampled, and were devoured by birds," He said. "Others were planted on rocky soil. When the plants came up, they withered because they had no moisture. Others were planted among thorn bushes. The thorn bushes grew up with them and choked them. Others were planted on good ground. When they came up, they produced a hundred times as much as was planted."

His disciples asked Him what the story meant. "This is what the story illustrates," Jesus answered. "The seed is God's Word. Some people are like the seeds that were planted along the road. They heard the Word, but then the devil comes. He takes the Word away from them so that they don't believe and become saved. Some people are like seeds on rocky soil. They welcome the Word with joy whenever they hear it, but they don't develop any roots. They believe for a while, but when their faith is tested, they abandon it. The seeds that were planted among thorn bushes are people who hear the Word, but as life goes on the worries, riches, and pleasures of life choke them. So they don't produce anything good. The seeds that were planted on good ground are people who also hear the Word. But they keep it in their good and honest hearts and produce what is good despite what life may bring."

The Word sown on the edge of the field is rejected by those who hear it. They simply do not believe God's saving message. Those persons on rocky soil seem to like what they hear but are without roots. Their faith dies. Faith begun among thorn bushes is squeezed out and choked by worries and the materialistic aspects of life. As a result, it becomes unproductive. Those who have received the Word on cultivated ground have strong faith and produce good fruit under all conditions.

A farmer with a **harvesting** mentality would choose only good ground. But that would cause much land and plants or trees to be ignored and relegated as useless. The wise church planter tends the entire acreage—all believers in the Church. Throughout scripture, spiritual leaders are encouraged to plant seeds and nurture them to maturity, not simply look for a harvest. More, the church farmer is to concentrate on the entire field, not just the productive acres.

THE SEED OF FAITH

The Seed-Word is the essence of Christian life. "Life is spiritual," Jesus said. "Your physical existence doesn't contribute to that life. The words that I have spoken to you are spiritual. They are life" (John 6:63). All spiritual renewal begins and ends with the Holy Spirit. It is the Spirit, through the Word, who reveals truth and enables a person to respond to it. Paul writes about the Father's ability to produce Christian desires and actions that please Him. He says that believers will not only grow, but shine like stars in the world as they "hold firmly to the Word of life" (Philippians 2:13-16).

The seed of God's Word is in every believer's heart. Each Christian is to become part of God's field, the Church. Scripture nourishes and waters the plant as it grows in the strength supplied by the Holy Spirit. The seed of the Word finds reception in the heart and develops. Germination is followed by growth. Growth culminates in fruit. Jesus said, "First the green blade appears, then the head, then the head full of grain" (Mark 4:28).

It is only by faith that minds, hearts, and lives—as well as personalities, abilities, voices, and time—can be implanted with this Word. Everything that a person is and does as a Christian is planted by faith into this life filled ground. Its health is expressed through witness and service to Christ through the Word. Like a grain of wheat, it will produce a hundredfold. If the Word is not planted on fertile soil, if it does not have the opportunity to become healthy, it will die without reproduction of any sort. It will die as a life that shows little or no purpose.

God wants His seed planted everywhere. The Holy Spirit alone causes that seed to sprout and grow (Mark 4:26-27). Paul says that neither he nor any other human is the one who causes it to sprout. God alone is the one who makes it grow (1 Corinthians 3:6-8). He is the one who gives the seed and the increase (2 Corinthians 9:10). The life-giving Word is powerful and productive. It will not go out without results. It accomplishes whatever God wants. It achieves whatever He sends it to do (Isaiah 55:10-11).

But the Word goes one step further. The message of Genesis stresses the fact that life perpetuates life. New life continues to develop from generation to generation. The capacity for reproduction is in fact the sign or proof of life. Life finds purpose and fulfillment in that reproduction. In the same way, spiritual reproduction gives purpose and fulfillment in the Christian life. Christians are to reproduce others who are just like themselves. The Word, as it works by the power of the Spirit, empowers Christians to bring others to spiritual maturity.

THE ORGANIC ESSENCE OF THE CHURCH

It is important to consider the organic nature of the Christian faith, both individually and in the Church. Jesus' parables about nature and agriculture did exactly that. He told about seeds that grow and of different types of soils. He talked about good and bad fruit and used illustrations that revolve around the seasons of sowing and reaping. In the Sermon on the Mount, Jesus asked His disciples to notice how the flowers grow in the field (Matthew 6:28). He was directing them to observe how God was more than capable of caring for everything in nature, as He does in His church.

In another story, Jesus told of a man who planted good seed in his field (Matthew 13:24-30). However, in that same field the man's enemy had planted weeds and secretly went away. This parable of nature becomes the believer's life story of grace. "The one who plants the good seed is the Son of Man. The field is the world. The good seeds are those who belong to the Kingdom" (Matthew 13:37-38). Jesus said that these people have God's approval—by His grace! They will shine like the sun in their Father's kingdom.

Jesus explained to them, "The weeds are those who belong to the evil one. The enemy who planted them is the devil. The harvest is the end of the world" (Matthew 13:38-39). At the end of all time the angels will gather these to be burned. The harvest belongs to One alone. All that is not of God will be rendered useless for eternity. On the other hand, those holding to faith in Jesus Christ will stand victoriously before the Throne of God.

GROWTH IS THE NATURE OF THE CHURCH

Growth is characteristic of and essential to the Church. Scripture is ripe with its growth analogies. After all, the nature and function of the Word is growth. Paul said, "The good news…is producing results and spreading all over the world as it did among you from the first day you heard it." Paul testified that growth exhibits itself in lives that prove the Lord's ownership. "You will want to please Him in every way as you grow in producing every kind of good work by the knowledge of God" (Colossians 1:6,10). This growth is true not only of the individual believer, but also of the entire Church. "Christ makes the whole body grow as God wants it to, through support and unity given by the joints and ligaments" (Colossians 2:19).

Again and again, the apostle Paul appealed to the Church to grow. He wanted the Philippian Christians to flourish and to be joyful in their faith (Philippians 1:25). He encouraged the Ephesians to be an entity that fits together and grows to be a holy temple in the Lord (Ephesians 2:21). He wanted the Corinthians to excel in their spiritual gifts in order that the Church might grow (1 Corinthians 14:12).

Paul acknowledged the spoken Word as an agent of growth. It is a necessary ingredient in the nurturing process. "When a person speaks what God has revealed," he said, "he speaks to people to help them grow, to encourage them, and to comfort them… When he speaks what God has revealed, he helps the church grow" (1 Corinthians 14: 3-4). This Word is powerful and able to produce results. When Paul recognized Christians who were bearing fruit, he was quick to commend their growth. "Your faith is active, your love is working hard, and your confidence in our Lord Jesus Christ is enduring" (1 Thessalonians 1:3). This was living evidence of growth!

Paul speaks of building up the body of Christ until it is mature and measures up to Christ Who is the standard. He says, "Then we will no longer be like children... Instead...we will grow up completely in our relationship to Christ, who is the head" (Ephesians 4: 13-15). God's will is that believers grow to full maturity in Christ. Peter says, "Desire God's pure Word as newborn babies desire milk. Then you will grow in your salvation" (1 Peter 2:2). In his second letter he says, "But grow in the good will and knowledge of our Lord and Savior Jesus Christ" (2 Peter 3:18).

The Book of Acts also provides many illustrations of growth. The Church grew in quality and quantity. Luke tells of its continual expansion. "The Word of God continued to spread, and the number of disciples in Jerusalem grew very large" (Acts 6:7). Even hardship led to growth. "The believers who were scattered went from place to place, where they spread the Word" (Acts 8:4). They boldly spread the good news of the Lord (Acts 8:25).

THE "AUTOMATIC GROWTH" PRINCIPLE

"Remember this," Paul said. "The farmer who plants a few seeds will have a very small harvest. But the farmer who plants because he has received God's blessings will receive a harvest of God's blessings in return" (2 Corinthians 9:6). Paul expected growth! He was certain that believers were entrusted to God and to His message of grace. "That message can help you grow," he said, "and can give you the inheritance that is shared by all of God's holy people" (Acts 20:32). Through the seed of the Word, the Church is planted, nurtured, and is constantly renewed so that it might grow. Through growth in that Word, the Church performs its mission task confidently.

In his book, **Natural Church Development**[1], Christian Schwarz speaks of the organic nature of the kingdom of God. Schwarz, who has studied over twenty-two thousand churches in fifty countries, calls it the **biotic** nature. "The biotic potential," he says, "is a concept designed by God the Creator Himself." Each local congregation has this natural capability. "We should not attempt to 'manufacture' church growth," he explains, "but rather to release the biotic potential which God has put into every church. It is our task to minimize the obstacles to church growth...both inside and outside the church."[2] "The release of God's growth automatisms is a strategic secret of growing churches."[3]

Schwarz calls Jesus' parable the "all by itself," or automatic growth principle. "The kingdom of God is like a man who scattered seeds on the ground," Jesus said. "He sleeps at night and is awake during the day. The seeds sprout and grow, although the man doesn't know how. The ground produces grain by itself. First the green blade appears, then the head, then the head full of grain. As soon as the grain is ready, he cuts it with a sickle, because harvest time has come" (Mark 4:26-29).

While the farmer's task is to plant and dutifully care for the field, it is God Who gives the increase. Servants of Christ cannot produce fruit. They cannot force growth. They only do what the Master has asked them to do—plant seeds, cultivate and fertilize. The servant must be patient as he awaits the harvest. Spiritual growth is a continual, gradual process that leads to maturity. The faith of each believer is to mature and multiply just as seeds are to sprout and grow. Only then does it bring forth an eternal harvest.

Schwarz draws a "principle-oriented" seed-planting approach from scripture. He suggests having no quantitative goals in a congregation's growth. Rather, he considers the **quality** of church life as the key to its development. "Natural church development," he says, "does not attempt to 'make' church growth, but to release the growth **automatisms** with which God Himself builds the church." Schwarz challenges churches to bid farewell to "superficial pragmatism, to simplistic cause-and-effect logic, to a fixation with quantity, to manipulative marketing methods. It means leaving behind human-made prescriptions to success and moving on to growth principles that are given by God Himself to all His creation."[4]

Technocratic methods do not get intended results. They look only at institutional or harvesting aspects of church growth. "The technocratic paradigm," Schwarz warns, "comes close to magical thinking. In the same way that a magician utters the magic words 'abracadabra' to bring about the desired results … automatically … so technocrats are utterly convinced that their formulas, dogmas, institutions or church growth programs will have a similar magical effect."[5]

One of the six organic biotic principles of nature that Schwarz applies to the church is **multiplication**. "A tree does not keep getting bigger," he affirms. "It brings forth new trees, which in turn produce more trees…. The principle of multiplication applies to all areas of church life: just as the true fruit of the apple tree is not an apple, but another tree; the true fruit of a small group is not another Christian, but another group; the true fruit of a church is not a new group, but a new church; the true fruit of a leader is not a follower, but a new leader; the true fruit of an evangelist is not a convert, but new evangelists. Whenever this principle is understood and applied, the results are dramatic – as can be shown empirically.... Reproduction through multiplication is simply a life principle of all God-created organisms, including the Church of Jesus Christ."[6]

Another organic biotic principle that Schwarz proclaims is **functionality**. "All living things in God's creation are characterized by their ability to bear fruit. Inherent to the nature of this fruit—be it an apple, a chestnut or even a baby—is the preservation of the species. Where there is no fruit, life is condemned to death. It is no accident that Jesus repeatedly referred to this natural law and applied it to the spiritual realm. In Matthew 7 we read, 'Every good tree bears good fruit' and 'you will know them by their fruits.'"[7]

CHRISTIANS AND CHURCHES THAT ARE BOTH HEALTHY AND PRODUCTIVE

Paul's letters show the organic nature of the church. This organic nature is the spirituality of the body of Christ. It does not need the bureaucracy or technology of a modern corporation. For the processes of planting seeds and nurture, Paul links growth with Christian calling and mission. He tells of healthy churches, unlike church systems in decline. They strive for ministry that relies on discipling and spiritual formation. They hold a solid commitment to biblical beliefs and values. These churches have a strong sense of the vision and mission to which God has called them. In Paul's eyes, servants of Christ and His Church are persons with a clearly articulated faith and spiritual life.

Were Paul here today, undoubtedly he would not be comfortable with declining church systems that are preoccupied with institutional membership. These types of churches are absorbed with **prescriptive thinking** that focuses on producing rites, committee formulas, and complex job descriptions. Rather, Paul's letters reveal leaders who demonstrate **descriptive thinking**. These leaders carefully balance both their productivity and accountability. They seek to grow permission-giving churches, ones that see a broad spectrum of ways in which God can work. Paul exemplified this type of strong spiritual leadership, not anything resembling the "machine management" of many traditional churches of our day.

Yes, ministries must be planted, cultivated and nurtured by Christ's servants. But Paul makes it clear that the work is not to glorify ourselves, but to glorify Christ. We do this as God's coworkers, doing God's work. "When some of you say, 'I follow Paul' and others say, 'I follow Apollos,' aren't you acting like sinful human beings?" Paul asks. "Who is Apollos?

Who is Paul? They are servants who help you come to faith. Each did what the Lord gave him to do. I planted, and Apollos watered, but God made it grow. So neither the one who plants nor the one who waters is important because only God makes it grow. The one who plants and the one who waters have the same goal, each will receive a reward for his own work. We are God's coworkers. You are God's field" (1 Corinthians 3:4-9). No matter which contribution is made to the whole of the work, "everything must be done to help each other grow" (1 Corinthians 14:26). Both the field and work are God's. They are fully of His doing.

If the church workers in Jesus' story are interpreted merely to be harvesters, His message is misunderstood. In Matthew 9, Jesus is the harvester on the Last Day. He saw troubled individuals who were helpless and lost. He felt sorry for the crowds and saw them as sheep without a shepherd. Jesus told his disciples, "The harvest is large, but the workers are few. So ask the Lord who gives this harvest to send workers to harvest His crops" (Matthew 9:37-38). It is not difficult to see that it is God who gives this harvest. It is likewise not difficult to see that God asks for workers. The big problem is that there are few workers who care for the field that has been seeded. The harvest depends on that cultivating.

The emphasis in Jesus' teaching was always that of being productive and healthy. "Do those things that prove you have turned to God and have changed the way you think and act," He said. Jesus criticized the Jews for depending upon their ancestry in Abraham instead of bearing fruit. "The ax is now ready to cut the roots of the trees," He warned. "Any tree that doesn't produce good fruit will be cut down and thrown into a fire" (Matthew 3:10).

Jesus named fruit as the criteria for measuring whether a person believed. "Not everyone who says to me, 'Lord, Lord!' will enter the kingdom of heaven," He said, "but only the person who does what My Father in heaven wants" (Matthew 7:21). "You will know them by what they produce," He said. "People don't pick grapes from thornbushes or figs from thistles, do they? In the same way every good tree produces good fruit, but a rotten tree produces bad fruit. A good tree cannot produce bad fruit, and a rotten tree cannot produce good fruit. Any tree that fails to produce good fruit is cut down and thrown into a fire. So you will know them by what they produce" (verses 16-19).

Simply stated, Jesus indicates that the Christian faith is not about easy talk, but about expressing faith in action. This fact does not alter the truth that believers are saved by grace through faith in Jesus Christ alone. As scripture affirms, good works contribute nothing toward salvation. But the Master desires that His servants produce worthwhile fruit, which is an expression of true faith. Jesus' words about the final judgment reveal His expectations for His servants. He holds them accountable for their works, the fruit of their faith. The real test will be whether Christian faith is turned into service to God and others, for Christians are known by their love.

Jesus challenged the Pharisees' traditions. He challenged their failure to do the will of the Father. Isaiah was right when he prophesied about them, saying, "These people honor me with their lips, but their hearts are far from me" (Matthew 15:8). Speaking directly of the Pharisees, Jesus said, "Any plant that my heavenly Father did not plant will be uprooted. Leave them alone! They are blind leaders … [they] will fall into the same pit" (Matthew 15:13-14). The religion of these failed leaders was neither healthy nor productive. Their self-centered works were of no lasting value in the kingdom of God.

PLANTED TO BEAR FRUIT

Christians are not left to bear fruit on their own. They are not called to give expression to their faith humanly by doing good works. The Word, however, is their water, the water that enables them to be strong in service and witness to Christ: "Rain and snow come down from the sky. They do not go back again until they water the earth. They make it sprout and grow so that it produces seed for farmers and food for people to eat. My Word, which comes from my mouth, is like the rain and snow. It will not come back to me without results. It will accomplish whatever I want and achieve whatever I send it to do" (Isaiah 55:10-11).

Jesus' story about the vine is one of the most instructive messages in the scriptures. John 15 is rich in agricultural images. "I am the true vine, and my Father takes care of the vineyard," Jesus taught. "He removes every one of my branches that doesn't produce fruit. He also prunes every branch that does not produce fruit to make it produce more fruit" (verse 1-2). The troubles and sicknesses Christians face are not punishment from God, but they are nevertheless used for His purposes. Just as pruning helps the vine to be more productive, the Father uses difficulties to rid believers of things that may be detrimental in their Christian walk. God uses the pruning to remove the "dead" wood—bad habits or harmful things—in their lives.

Through the Word, Jesus demonstrates that Christians will be able to bear fruit as they live in Him. "Live in me, and I will live in you. A branch cannot produce any fruit by itself. It has to stay attached to the vine. In the same way, you cannot produce fruit unless you live in me. I am the vine. You are the branch. Those who live in me while I live in them will produce a lot of fruit, but you cannot produce anything without me. Whoever doesn't live in me is thrown away like a branch and dries up. Branches like this are gathered, thrown into a fire and burned. If you live in me and what I say lives in you, then ask for anything you want and it will be yours. You give glory to my Father when you produce a lot of fruit and therefore show that you are my disciples" (John 15: 4-8).

Jesus says that doing good works is not a choice: "You didn't choose Me, but I chose you. I have appointed you to go, to produce fruit that will last, and ask the Father in my name to give you whatever you ask for" (John 15: 16). The request which the believer makes to the heavenly Father, however, is not for a Mercedes or a mansion. The Christian asks for the will to serve his or her purpose faithfully as a strong servant of the Lord.

Paul, addressing the Christians at Galatia, impressed upon them the importance of planting good seeds in their daily lives. "Make no mistake about this: You can never make a fool out of God. Whatever you plant is what you will harvest. If you plant in the soil of your corrupt nature, you will harvest destruction. But if you plant in the soil of your spiritual nature, you will harvest eternal life. We can't allow ourselves to get tired of living the right way. Certainly, each of us will receive everlasting life at the proper time, if we don't give up. Whenever we have the opportunity, we have to do what is good for everyone, especially for the family of believers" (Galatians 6:7-10). Paul reminds each Christian to be productive in ministry. Each believer is a planter responsible for the individual seed he or she sows.

Jesus taught a lesson to those preparing the way for the Gospel. As their pay, those who sow and harvest will see new believers enter the kingdom. "The person who harvests the crop is already getting paid. He is gathering grain for eternal life. So the person who plants the grain and the person who harvests it are to be together. In this respect, the saying is true: 'One person plants, and another person harvests.' I have sent you to harvest a crop you have not worked for. Other people have done the hard work and you have followed them in their work" (John 4:36-38).

SPIRITUAL FORMATION—SHAPED BY THE WORD

What is the nature and purpose of God's seed, the Word? Unless we understand major obstacles in reading and understanding the Word, the message may not be received. These obstacles may cause mere information to be transmitted without the Word doing its work of spiritual formation. It is so easy to settle for head knowledge that does not reach the heart. It is God's desire that those who read His Word receive His personal message. He wants to address and heal real needs.

M. Robert Mulholland, Jr., in his book *Shaped by the Word*[8] emphasizes the power of scripture in the process of spiritual formation. He identifies three major obstacles that keep believers held captive by cultural forms. The first barrier is that of reading scripture in a personal way that reduces it to an echo of one's own self-image. This type of reading fails to see the person of God as a "word" spoken from Him. The second barrier is dealing manipulatively with the text on the basis of having a conscious or unconscious agenda. That agenda addresses the text rather than being addressed by it. This obstacle causes the reader to control the text rather than it instructing the Christian. The third obstacle is that of having a wrong view of the Bible. The reader does not accept its true nature as the inherent, written Word of God. He or she treats scripture as little more than mere information.

These three obstacles may hinder readers from receiving the full message God wants to deliver. They can cause the reading of scripture to merely "tinker" with a present system of understanding and values. On the surface, structures of life may be reordered and the dynamics of the ways things are done may be modified, but the Christian still remains locked into the old self-generated self. The possibility of miraculous spiritual formation is removed.

The purpose of the Bible is not merely to provide information for doctrine and salvation. 2 Timothy 3:16-17 does not stop at the words, "Every scripture passage is inspired by God." It goes on to say, "All of them are useful for teaching, pointing out errors, correcting people, and training them for a life that has God's approval. They equip God's servants so that they are completely prepared to do good things." Doctrinal truths are not to be learned at the expense of growing in maturity. The Christian demonstrates scripture's effect by modeling a trust-filled faith and a faith-filled life.

The Word is to transform minds and lives! Paul uplifts the Word as actually having an incarnational attribute that makes Christians "living letters." Romans 12:1-2 says that because of God's compassion toward them, believers are to offer their bodies as living sacrifices, dedicated to Him and pleasing to Him. They are to change the way they think so that they "will always be able to determine what God really wants—what is good, pleasing and perfect." To be formed in Christ is a gift of God. God gave His Word to call us into relationship with its author and, in so doing, to form His people in the image of Christ. Yes, information is vital for spiritual formation, but only when clearly and properly presented as the work of the Holy Spirit. It is He who transforms.

It is a fact that many persons interpret scripture through the lens of traditional thought patterns and church practices. Information-seeking and behavior dynamics are deeply ingrained into the human nature. These patterns and dynamics automatically take over and blind many who hear or read the Word. The focus, however, must be on the transformation through the Word, on how the Master desires to change His servants to be more and more like Him. Raw human nature wants the rights of the kingdom without obedience to the King. The King sees the reverse to be true.

Mulholland goes on to share his concerns regarding obstacles that center on the **doing** of Christian duties rather than the **being** of a Christian in ministry. If the doing of Christian duties and the maintenance of the church are central in the reading of scripture, those tasks will be used as a means to accomplish our own agenda. If these are the goal, scripture becomes a tool for personal purposes and desires. A façade of church activities is constructed which tends to be mistaken for genuine spirituality. Lists of "do's and don'ts" continually expand while the inner being shrinks. Spiritual formation, rather, is the process of being conformed to the image of Christ. This formation takes place first at the being level, the relational level, not the doing level. Thoughts, emotions, actions and dynamics of relationships are the arenas where, bit-by-bit, by the Word, Christian character is shaped and strengthened.

Mulholland writes, "The very thought of being 'conformed'—which clearly implies that we are to be grasped, controlled, and shaped by someone other than ourselves—militates against our deeply ingrained sense of being. 'Graspers' powerfully resist being grasped by God. Controllers are inherently incapable of yielding control to God. Manipulators strongly reject being shaped by God."[9]

Mulholland states that we earthbound beings build, maintain, and defend a complex structure of habits and attitudes. Their perceptions of personal and corporate relationships, as well as the dynamics created by them, become patterns of reaction and response towards each situation encountered. On the positive side, these patterns enable human beings to cope with life. But this complex structure "becomes an ever-thickening crust of 'self' that severely imprisons and limits the individual. It tends to garble and distort the unique calling God has bestowed on each believer through His Word. This complex structure can debase the person, causing him or her to doubt God's truth concerning individual worth in God's eyes. It prevents the Christian from recognizing who he or she was created to be in Christ. Established patterns prevent growth into wholeness. They thwart the process of God's intent for the individual to be shaped by the living Word of God."[10]

The use of information and methods in the present culture facilitates regulation and control. It does so for the church as well as for all of life. It causes a church to be seen as a personal structure, in personal terms. God's grace, however, seeks to liberate His people from this destructive bondage. His Holy Spirit seeks to create in them, in their being and character, a whole new structure of habits, attitudes, and relationships. He seeks to create in them new responses to His Word. His grace powerfully works through His Word. Yes, they learn of inconsistencies in their Christian character. But they also learn that they are offered loving nurture into the holiness so much needed—and the grace to change and act.

Spiritual formation results when a person embraces the biblical perception of being a "living letter" that God speaks in the world. The sin-distorted "word" of self is then reshaped by the power of the **living** Word. What then is the purpose of reading scripture? It is that Christians increasingly become what they already are in Christ! Where change is needed, excuses will not make it. Neither will feverish actions in an attempt to "pay" for sins and guilt. Rather, repentance and forgiveness in Christ are required.

The Word is the vehicle of God's light to search hearts. "God's word is living and active. It is sharper than any two-edged sword and cuts as deep as the place where soul and spirit meet, the place where joints and marrow meet. God's word judges a person's thoughts and intentions…everything is uncovered and exposed for Him to see. We must answer to Him" (Hebrews 4:12-13). Only the living Word brings a proper perspective regarding individual believers and each church. Only the living Word gives clear direction for tending God's field and taking the next step.

SPIRITUAL FORMATION SHOULD BE THE MAIN OBJECTIVE OF SUNDAY SCHOOLS AND BIBLE CLASSES

The scene in many Sunday schools and Bible classes is one of lecturing with a few questions by the students with little awareness of how few are really learning. Few ask questions about what is happening and whether what they are doing is working. As a result, knowledge is added, but there is little spiritual formation. Many employ models and procedures that have changed little over time. George Barna said, "Sunday schools simply do not provide the quality of teaching and experience that people demand these days in exchange for their time."[11] Life patterns and the learning culture have changed, but most Sunday schools and Bible classes have not. It is not surprising that a third grader said, "The teacher just talks and we just sit there."[12]

Education through interactive Bible study for spiritual formation should be the church's most potent tool for growing its people. Instead, outdated educational systems and approaches are the root cause of member apathy. Instead of learners, members are often victims of a poor system. Most churches have the assumption that if we are teaching, the people must be learning. "There is a general assumption that teaching should result in learning and that learning is a consequence of teaching," writes Professor Frank Smith in his book *Insult to Intelligence*. "The problem with this assumption is that the student tends to be blamed for failure to learn. The thought is rarely entertained that teachers might not be teaching what they think they are teaching."[13]

Interactive learning allows the learners to discover truth and take advantage of teachable moments. It occurs basically in the learners' context. Interactive learning is student-based, not teacher-based, and promotes positive interdependence. It encourages spiritual formation and building of relationships instead of merely adding knowledge. Only those who dig deeper into scriptures through interactive study, requiring students to do homework and to share their findings in the group discussion will experience real spiritual formation. Possibly 20 percent of congregations are like this.

PROPER NUTRITION AND NURTURE RAISES CHRISTIANS WHO PRODUCE

Flourishing farms and flourishing churches run on the same principles. Whether farmer's field or God's field, each plant is to be cultivated, fertilized, and nurtured. If healthy formation and growth are desired, each believer needs to be fed.

The scripture overview presented in this chapter reveals agricultural principles seen in the teachings of both Jesus and Paul. But it also highlights the profound comparison between farmer Jim's intense concentration on the health and productivity of all his plants and a church leader's urgent responsibility and accountability to major on the health and productivity of all of God's people. The pastor and his appointed leaders are to feed God's people, tending to His field for deep spiritual formation.

Like Jim's motivation in planting, the apostle Paul emphasizes the importance of church leaders motivating members to be productive. "Remember this," Paul says, "the farmer who plants a few seeds will have a very small harvest. But the farmer who plants because he has received God's blessings will receive a harvest of God's blessings in return…God will give you His constantly overflowing kindness. Then, when you always have everything you need, you can do more and more things…God gives seed to the farmer and food to those who need to eat. God will also give you seed and multiply it. In your lives you will increase the things you do that have His approval. God will make you rich enough so that you will always be generous" (2 Corinthians 9: 6, 8, 10-11).

Paul's words illustrate the intimate relationship between God and His spiritual "farmers" – His people. He speaks to them candidly about the use of their God-given resources. God has given these resources to be used for His purposes and for His glory. What He gives is to be carefully invested—not hidden, consumed, misused or thrown away. God's resources, whether physical or spiritual, are to be used as He intended— to produce abundantly more crops and fruit.

CHAPTER 4

The Dimensions and Goals of a Seed-Planting Church

Each church has a choice whether it wants to have church "ala carte"—growing piece by piece, committee by committee, program by program—or whether it wants to be Christ's natural community of faith. Does the church leader want a "plastic" organization built by various boards in the church? Does he want to follow years, even centuries, of traditions and program formation? Or does the leader want an organic, "elastic" church guided creatively by the Holy Spirit through the Word?

THE DIMENSIONS OF AN ORGANIC CHURCH

How are the dimensions of an organic church defined, driven, developed, directed and distinguished?

1. *The nurturing church is **defined** by its planting and nurturing.* Farmer Jim concentrated intensely on every aspect of planting and nurturing. Likewise, Jesus and Paul proclaimed and expounded on the same. The healthy church is defined by them. The Church is basically about seeding and nurturing, not harvesting.

The nurturing congregation determines its essential nature (DNA) and knows it well. It understands every aspect of this DNA and communicates it clearly. It tends its members with quality and purpose through the Word and Sacraments. The organic church recognizes that Jesus alone is the divine Harvester on the Last Day.

2. *The nurturing church is **driven** by the Gospel of Jesus Christ.* Its message is God's grace, balanced with His loving expectations, proclaimed in repentance and forgiveness through the Lord Jesus Christ. Jesus Himself described the intensity of the gospel message (Luke 24:46-47).

The healthy congregation is inspired, compelled, and empowered by Jesus Christ Himself. It is He who sends every believer to work in the Father's field. It is His compassionate love that is the driving power of the mission. "Clearly, Christ's love guides us…He died for all people so that those who live will no longer live for themselves but for the man who died and was brought back to life for them… So from now on we don't think of anyone from a human point of view… God has done all this. He has restored our relationship with Him through Christ and has given us this ministry of restoring relationships" (2 Corinthians 5: 14-16, 18). It is this gospel that drives the nurturing church.

3. *The nurturing church is **developed** by the Seed as food and water.* The ministry of the church is spiritually built and formed through the use of God's Word. That Seed brings the congregation into being, expands it, and continually influences it in its ministry of discipling. Instead of saying that the **churches** grew in Acts 6:7, Paul states, "The word of God continued to spread, and the number of disciples in Jerusalem grew very large." He relates the same fact in Acts 12:24, "But God's word continued to spread and win many followers." Bible study as well as leaders who are trained on the basis of the Word are key factors in developing a healthy church.

4. *The nurturing church is **directed** by the Great Commission.* Jesus Christ sends His people out into the field. The healthy congregation carries out the mandate of His commission: "All authority in heaven and on earth has been given to me. So wherever you go, make disciples of all nations: Baptize them in the name of the Father, and of the Son, and of the Holy Spirit. Teach them to do everything I have commanded you. And remember that I am always with you until the end of time" (Matthew 28: 18-20). This is a task of disciple-making, teaching and evangelizing.

The absence of disciple-making and evangelizing is a fatal defect in any church. People are not classified as disciples just because they go to church and are involved in a Christian activity. The call to discipleship is not a "week-end hobby," but rather a life-long commitment to obey the Great Commission. The disciple's vision is to work together to share Christ's love with a Great Commission passion.

5. *The nurturing church is **distinguished** by its biblical "delivery system."* The healthy church conveys its spiritual resources effectively to every point of need. It is an "equipping church" that prepares leaders and members for their individual ministries. This church looks for every

opportunity to plant, feed, and water. It has a delivery team comprised of biblically equipped leaders and workers. Each person is trained, encouraging all believers to " bloom where he or she is planted." The church's basic strategy is founded on God's principle of nurture. The healthy church creates intentional pathways to growth. It concentrates on the congregation's mission, not the size of the parish.

The nurturing church employs a scripture-centered system that is conducive to disciple-making. The leadership team is thoroughly equipped to sow and cultivate. It has the task to tend and nourish all persons in the field. Leaders are not satisfied until the congregation is transformed into a seed-planting, nurturing church. They make certain that the biblical delivery system is constructed to promote life-bearing multiplication.

Leaders in the healthy church seek to grow a body that is spiritually alive at the same time as being culturally relevant. They mobilize it for a ministry that is united in Spirit. The leaders plant and grow workers who express compassion for each person while being sensitive to the needs of all people. They move the ministry forward in aggressive outreach. The leaders are bold to evangelize the lost and to plant churches. They select and gather leaders, equipping and empowering them for God's mission. They integrate and align God's resources for new and growing ministries.

THE BIBLICAL BASIS FOR A NURTURING, EQUIPPING CHURCH

The healthy church is built upon the equipping principles found in Paul's letters to Timothy and the church in Ephesus. The leadership principle found in 2 Timothy 2:2 is basic to a healthy, functioning church: "You've heard my message," Paul says, "and it's been confirmed by many witnesses. Entrust this message to faithful individuals who will be competent to teach others" (2 Timothy 2:2). The task of faithful leaders is to develop disciples who are able to disciple others. Making disciples is the first principle of leadership development and membership maturation. It is the foundational precept of the *divine system*.

Built upon the principle he had written to Timothy, Paul further expounds the *divine system* of disciple-making to the Ephesians: "I…encourage you to live the kind of life that proves that God has called you…God's favor [grace] has been given to each of us. It is measured out by Christ who gave it…He also gave…pastors and teachers as gifts to His church. Their purpose is to prepare God's people, to serve, and to build up the body of Christ. This is to continue until all of us are united in our faith and in our knowledge about God's Son, until we become mature, until we measure up to Christ, who is the standard. Then we will no longer be little children, tossed and carried about by all kinds of teachings that change like the wind. We will no longer be influenced by people who use cunning and clever strategies to lead us astray. Instead, as we lovingly speak the truth, we will grow up completely in our relationship with Christ, who is the head. He makes the whole body fit together and unites it through the support of every joint. As each and every part does its job, He makes the body grow so that it builds itself up in love" (Ephesians 4:1,7,11-16). The nurturing, equipping church recognizes and employs Ephesians 4 as the basis for growing productive and fruit-bearing Christians.

THE DIVINE SYSTEM

What exactly is this *divine system*? What does it entail? Upon what is it based? Scripture highlights six principles that define the system as ordained by God.

1. *God calls His people to life-long ministry.* God's **call** is actually twofold—first to salvation, then to sanctification. "You will know the confidence that He calls you to have," Paul writes, "and the glorious wealth that God's people will inherit" (Ephesians 1:18). This amazing call to salvation is rich with present and eternal benefits: "We were dead because of our failures," Paul goes on, "but He made us alive together with Christ. (It is God's kindness that saved you.) God has brought us back to life together with Christ Jesus and has given us a position in heaven with him. He did this through Christ Jesus out of His generosity to us in order to show His extremely rich kindness in the world to come. God saved you through faith as an act of kindness (grace). You had nothing to do with it. Being saved is a gift from God. It's not the result of anything you've done, so no one can brag about it" (Ephesians 2:5-9).

The call to sanctification is clearly stated in God's Word. Ephesians 2:10 says, "God has made us what we are. He has created us in Christ Jesus to live lives filled with good works that He has prepared for us to do." Paul's encouragement is direct in telling us to "live the kind of life which proves that God has called you" (Ephesians 4:1). God's call is not to church voluntarism or helping to meet a budget, but to answer His call to be a faithful servant and witness of the Lord Jesus Christ.

2. *God's people minister on the basis of grace and the gifts He has given.* God is not asking His people to do or give anything that He has not already supplied. "God's favor (grace) has been given to each of us.

It was measured out to us by Christ who gave it" (Ephesians 4:7). When God calls persons to ministry, He gives the resources for them to be able to minister and serve.

Grace, even in the midst of doctrinal orthodoxy, has been distorted in church practice. Biblical knowledge has often been allowed to remain merely a mental process, rather than something applied or related to life. People are left with head knowledge that does not touch the heart. Sanctification and good works become confused when the churches and leaders allow various negative factors to be present. In a faulty response to the Word, rituals can easily replace Christian love and action. Church members may replace personal piety with church activities. They may not understand the proper linkage between justification and sanctification. There may actually be a fear of the words "obey" and "obedience," believing that they connote some sort of legalism. This is in spite of the fact that Jesus said, if anyone loves Him, that person would obey His commandments.

Some church members may fear that an emphasis on good works will crowd out the message of salvation by grace through faith in Jesus. As a result, they fail to adequately stress Paul's clear indicatives and imperatives concerning these same good works. The church may stress Christology to the exclusion of the Holy Spirit's work and the Father's providence. In short, the distinction between the primary motivation (Christ's love) and a secondary motivation (gratitude to God and fear of Him) of the Christian life is unclear.

The result can be "cheap grace," as Dietrich Bonhoeffer recounts in *The Cost of Discipleship*. "Cheap grace" (grace without relation to the context of living) is a system of intellectual ascent that clouds the matter of forgiveness of sins and fruits of repentance and righteousness.

Use of the Spirit's gifts results in healthy Christians and healthy churches. Paul said, "I don't want there to be any misunderstanding concerning spiritual gifts" (1 Corinthians 12:1). Still, many churches know little or nothing about this grace given by God for ministry. Every Christian should know that there "are different spiritual gifts, but the same Spirit gives them. There are different ways of serving, yet the same Lord is served. There are different types of work to do, but the same God produces every gift in every person. The evidence of the Spirit's presence is given to each person for the common good of everyone" (1 Corinthians 12: 4-7).

As an example, Paul notes that the Spirit gives one person the ability to speak with wisdom while He gives another courageous faith. "There is only one Spirit who does all these things by giving what God wants to give to each person" (1 Corinthians 12: 8-11), he says. Peter echoes the same, "Each of you as a good manager should use the gift that God has given you to serve others. Whoever speaks must speak God's words. Whoever serves must serve with the strength God supplies so that in every way God receives glory through Jesus Christ" (1 Peter 4:10-11).

The nature of the church demands that God's people understand these spiritual gifts or "grace gifts." What is the Church? It is God's people ministering to each other according to their unique God-given gifts. Each spiritual gift is a unique capacity given by the Holy Spirit to a believer for ministry and service in Christ's church.

All gifts must be used to build up the body. Paul gives useful suggestions in Romans 12:6-8: "God in his kindness (grace) gave each of us different gifts. If your gift is speaking God's word, make sure what you say agrees with the Christian faith. If your gift is serving, then devote yourself to serving. If it is teaching, then devote yourself to teaching. If it is encouraging others, devote yourself to giving encouragement. If it is sharing, be generous. If it is leadership, lead enthusiastically. If it is helping people in need, help them cheerfully."

Healthy, nurturing churches assist Christians to serve in their area of giftedness. They help each "priest" to identify and develop his or her specific gifts. In doing so, they enable them to function as servants of Jesus Christ by the power of the Holy Spirit. God's calling and spiritual giftedness are essential elements of the Christian's life in the Church. Each is to do his or her work as a minister of God—whether pastoral or in a lay capacity. Simply stated, it is each believer's task to discover, develop and use all spiritual gifts for service in Christ's kingdom.

With the wide variety of books and resources available on spiritual gifts, church leaders will first want to study those from their own denomination. There are others that may be helpful. One that is worthy of review is *"GRASP" Spiritual Gifts for Christian Ministry and Service*. Part of the lay ministry package, *Getting a GRASP on your Personal Mission*, the acronym *GRASP* guides church members to discover God's purpose and call in their lives for Christ.

CHAPTER 4

G—Groundings: Christian beliefs and values that guide a believer to his purpose

R—Role: Services and activities in which a Christian excels

A—Abilities: Competence or talent that comes naturally to a person

S—Spiritual gifts: Unique capabilities bestowed on a Christian by grace

P—Passion: Fire or zeal that fuels a person's desire to serve God with his gifts

God's Word does not outline a definite plan on how to discover spiritual gifts. It does however instruct the believer to discover, develop, and use them for the building of His church. A careful use of a gifts discovery inventory can be effective to assist the congregation to fulfill its mission. The spiritual gifts tool *GRASP* is one of those that can help to identify unique gifts, callings, and passion in the church.[1] Applying the words of Jesus Christ to daily living, believers are enabled to find meaning and God-given purpose in life. *GRASP* is a tool for believers to discern God's call on their lives and to discover the skills and resources they possess.

God's gifts come in all sizes—some large, some small. The only difference is that His spiritual gifts are found *in* people—young and old, male and female, educated and uneducated. The tragedy is that apparently many Christians either do not recognize their gifts or do not open them. Seed-planting leaders will help people recognize unopened gifts. They will teach them to open gifts and use them according to God's instructions.

The parable of the talents relays valuable instruction on using gifts, whether a believer has been given ten, four, or two. The one given ten gifts doubled his investment. He was told, "Good job! You're a good and faithful servant! You proved that you could be trusted with a small amount. I will put you in charge of a larger amount. Share your master's happiness." The one who received four gifts doubled his investment and was likewise told he was faithful and could be trusted: "I will put you in charge of a large amount. Come and share your master's happiness" (Matthew 25:14-23).

The servant who received two gifts dug a hole and hid them in the ground. When the master returned, this steward told him, "Sir, I knew that you were a hard person to please. You harvest where you haven't planted and gather where you haven't scattered any seed. I was afraid. So I hid your two thousand dollars in the ground. Here's your money!"

His master responded, "If you knew that I harvested where I haven't planted and gathered where I haven't scattered, then you should have invested my money with the bankers. When I returned, I would have received my money back with interest" (Matthew 25:24-27). God does not approve of buried talents and unused spiritual gifts. He is not pleased when they are unused or spent on anything that is harmful and destructive. He has lovingly and extravagantly supplied them for ministry.

For this reason, it is important that every church should plan some sort of spiritual gift employment strategy. It must create some sort of a placement system in which every member, new or long-term, participates in a biblical study of spiritual gifts. Each believer must learn how to identify, develop, and utilize his or her spiritual gifts for the good of God's kingdom.

Pastors and leaders must lay a proper foundation and cast the vision for spiritual gifts. This can be done by a series of sermons on the subject. Some of the specific aspects covered would be:

(1) Every Christian has a gift and is to use it. 1 Peter 4:10; Ephesians 4:7

(2) People have different gifts. Romans 12: 6; 1 Corinthians 12:28-30

(3) All gifts are important for ministry. 1 Corinthians 12:4-11

(4) The Church is a body where all parts are to work together. 1 Corinthians 12:12-27; Ephesians 4:16

(5) Pastors and teachers equip people for ministry. Ephesians 4:11-12

Another possibility would be for the congregation to consider holding a "Gift Night" or a "Gift Workshop" for all members. This evening or workshop would then be offered to new members annually. No matter by which means, a congregation continually must share its vision that all church members, as disciples of Jesus Christ, are meant to minister on the basis of the gifts given them by the Holy Spirit. Each person should learn how he or she can become involved and make a difference for Christ.

A scripturally based spiritual gifts inventory should offer ministry opportunities in the church and determine what gift-mix contributes to effectiveness in that work. Ministry tasks can be identified with specific spiritual gifts. Interviews are a critical step in the placement process. The best task placements are made by conducting face-to-face interviews.

Various questions can be raised during the interview. "How do you understand spiritual gifts?" "What is their importance in your ministry to God?" "What in Christ's kingdom touches your heart and makes it beat faster?" "Have you been involved in ministry in other churches and in other organizations?" "What were your roles in them?" "Have you identified your spiritual gift and how you may minister with it?"

    3. *Leaders are to fulfill their God-given purpose of preparing people to serve.* God's call to pastors and teachers is to teach and instruct. They must know that in order to serve, God's call on members is first a call to learn and be taught in the Word. "Their purpose is to prepare God's people, to serve, and to build up the body of Christ" (Ephesians 4:12).

The traditional, harvesting church has built a volunteer system without adequate concern for fully preparing the people for ministry. This volunteer system is based primarily on matching skills with tasks, not spiritual gifts with ministries. It is characterized by leaders giving an appeal for church workers rather than a distinct call from God. As a result, enthusiasts use their skills well while the majority of persons are spectators who watch them. The major problem is that few of God's people are anywhere near the place where true preparation is happening. They simply are not where the teaching and training is occurring (Ephesians 4:12). True, a church can be maintained and survive with half its members active, one-quarter of them marginal, the other quarter inactive. But under such conditions, the body of Christ can not be built, nor is the divine system embraced.

    When the teaching and equipping principles of Ephesians 4:12 are practiced, the church will be an active seed-planting, nurturing church. When these discipling principles are ignored, it will be a maintenance, harvesting church. Pastors and church leaders have a choice—follow God's design or the traditional road.

    4. *Intensive discipling is to continue until there is unity of faith and spiritual maturity.* How long are God's people to be nurtured and equipped for ministry? "This is to continue until all of us are united in our faith and in our knowledge about God's Son. Until we become mature, until we measure up to Christ, who is the standard" (Ephesians 4:13).

    Confirmation and membership classes are not a graduation, but an entrance into lifelong Bible study. The Word brings maturity and enables lives to measure up to Christ, who is the standard. It unites believers in faith, the kind needed to do the ministry of building up the body of Christ and evangelizing the world. This lifelong nutritional requirement, the "diet" of the Word, should not be any more surprising than the physical body's need for daily food.

This spiritual reality is faithfully practiced by healthy churches. The harvesting church, however, or any church that ignores the basic discipling function found in Paul's letter, will have too many immature members. These persons fit the description found in Ephesians 4:14. They will be "little children, tossed and carried about by all kinds of teachings that change like the wind." They will be "influenced by people who use cunning and clever strategies" and be led astray.

5. *The believer's relationship to Christ grows as all lovingly speak the truth.* "As we lovingly speak the truth, we will grow up completely in our relationship to Christ, who is the head" (Ephesians 4:15). Lovingly speak the truth to another person? When Jesus taught deep truths about Himself as food and bread for believers, many of His disciples said, "What He says is hard to accept. Who wants to listen to Him anymore?" (John 6:60).

Ephesians 4:15 is another of those difficult teachings. Many are fearful of it because it seems far too demanding. The culture in America, as well as others around the world, simply does not choose to become involved in anything that risky. Most church members observing errant behavior by family members and others in the church do nothing. By ignoring the behavior, they communicate the fact that everyone should mind his or her own business. "I don't want to get involved in that," they say. "Who am I to say anything?" Or they might say, "That's the elders' and deacons' business." At the same time, elders and deacons often will not touch the situation because there are others in the church who would not appreciate this "correction."

But the words of scripture are as plain as can be: As Christians lovingly speak the truth, "we will grow up completely in our relationship with Christ" (Ephesians 4:15). Any failure to lovingly speak the truth results in church members remaining weak. It results in persons "playing church" instead of being the church. Church members then remain undistinguished from the rest of the world. There is little difference between their visible lifestyle and that of their neighbors.

This exhortation to speak the truth is given to all believers in a congregation, not solely to their pastors or elders and deacons. This failure becomes a fatal flaw in the life of the congregation. An important part of living "the kind of life which proves that God has called you," (4:1) is to lovingly speak the truth.

The church does not need condemnations and legalistic lectures that try to correct any situation. But it does need to equip and prepare God's people for the ministry of speaking the truth. Nothing in this teaching indicates that the matter of every believer lovingly speaking the truth is up for a vote by a church council or assembly. No vote or debate is needed, only obedience. The commitment for all people to "lovingly speak the truth" to each other begins with an acknowledgment that this is every member's responsibility. Leaders must then begin to equip God's people by enlisting them in Bible studies. The Word and the Spirit will gain them one by one.

6. *In God's divine equipping and discipling system, every believer is involved in ministry.* This divine system is described in Ephesians 4:16. "He makes the whole body fit together and unites it through the support of every joint. As each and every part does its job, he makes the body grow so that it builds itself up in love."

Effective ministry is not engineered by church leaders. The church does not grow because some gifted church leader organized a master plan. Ephesians 4 shows that *God* makes the church grow. Verse 16 tells that it is *He* who makes the whole body fit together and unites it through the support of believers whom He has called and gifted for ministry. Focusing on the church as the body of Christ, God says this fitting together and working together is accomplished through the support of every joint-member – not 35% or 60% of the members. It is the cooperation of every member that makes everyone fit for service.

1 Corinthians 12 informs us how this happens. God makes the body grow so that it builds itself up in love as each and every part does its job. That task is not one assigned by pastors or church leaders, but is given by God's grace and His gifting to each person. "The evidence of the Spirit's presence is given to each person for the common good of everyone" (1 Corinthians 12:7). *Each and every part or member* has been given a gift for ministry to the whole body. This may sound foreign in the practice of the traditional harvesting church. It will not match up to the usual volunteer activities done by a small percentage of the membership. But the Church must face the *divine system!*

In most congregations, only a small percentage of believers use their God-given, grace-bestowed spiritual gifts. Very few give support to the whole body through any type of ministry. When we consider that fact, it is literally a miracle that the Church, as the body of Christ, has not been crippled to the point of non-function. It is amazing to see the good that does happen in traditional, harvesting churches operating under a more human approach. This gives credit to the power of the gospel and the Spirit of God even in spite of a church's endeavors to do the job through too many human efforts.

Jesus and Paul taught by using pictures of life and growth. Their messages often made analogies to farmers and crops. They echoed the same organic type of body-life found in Ephesians 4:16. The entire chapter reveals the true characteristic of the seed-planting, nurturing church. This scriptural teaching, of course, is in stark contrast to the human "synthetic" approach found in many harvesting churches.

Ephesians 4:16 pictures every member fruitfully functioning in the body. In contrast, a harvesting church finds only about 20-35% of members doing any works of service. Most members give only token service in helping the church complete its projects and programs. In a sense, the equipping approach of the church described in Ephesians is spiritually "professional," while the other is spiritually untrained and amateurish. In another sense, the first bears fruit that is grown naturally on the tree or plant, while the other sometimes "wears" fruit, somewhat like ornaments hung on a Christmas tree.

A church becomes a nurturing church when members develop spiritual minds that have been instructed by the Word. A church becomes a harvesting church, however, when its leaders imitate techniques and formulas that are meant to produce "churchly" results. In Ephesians, Paul outlines the divine system, while the other system is nothing more than a human model with some Biblical components.

After careful study of Ephesians 4, especially verse sixteen, there is one primary encouragement: *Don't try to beat the system!* For the seventeen centuries since Constantine institutionalized the church, the traditional harvesting church has basically been "trying to beat the system."

Even though Paul's words are directed to personal piety, they are fitting for church leaders. "So I tell you and encourage you in the Lord's name not to live any longer like other people in the world" (Ephesians 4:17). Leaders dare not lead with worldly minds and technocratic plans. They are not merely church CEOs, but God's particular people called to function faithfully in the body. They have God's call to God's system. That call includes the Spirit's strength and wisdom needed in order to use it.

The equipping and nurturing church has Ephesians 4 as its operating plan. It functions on the basis of the divine ministry system. God calls.

God gives grace and gifts to act. He supplies pastors and teachers to prepare His people for ministry. He continues to grow people until they measure up to the standard of Christ. God makes the whole body fit together and unites it through the ministry of every believer, as each one uses his or her gifts. God makes the body grow so that it builds itself up in love.

Has our congregation heard God's call? Is ours the *divine system* or our system?

CHAPTER 5

Abundant Stewardship Harvests Come From Abundant Planting And Nurturing

There is no shortage of money in the church. There is, however, a lack of good stewardship training. Grace-filled sermons and Bible studies on Christian giving are also scarce. Churches have many fruit-pickers but not enough persons willing to do the digging and fertilizing necessary to grow a healthy, productive tree. People are led to believe that they are good stewards when (1) they meet their individual pledge, (2) give a large sum, (3) the congregational yearly budget goal is achieved, or (4) the church has finished a particular fund-raising project. Many times, these goals have been achieved without making any reference to proportionate giving; to giving a set percentage to God.

Two disparate approaches characterize church giving programs—the traditional (programmatic) approach and the scriptural (nurturing) approach. Traditional stewardship programs are based on maintenance—giving "to" a budget. They look at certain requirements that dictate what each person is to give in order to maintain the church's programs. Scriptural stewardship, on the other hand, is a "from" or missional approach. Based on the concept of the priesthood, every Christian is a priest of God. Each believer gives **from** what God has so graciously given.

There must be a significant fundamental change in thought and function:

	CHANGE FROM	**CHANGE TO**
1	Stewardship programs that target increases in contributions	Stewardship education in strengthening spiritual life and fruitfulness
2	Church gifts given in order to meet church bills	Worshipful living that compels persons to bring their lives and gifts to the altar
3	Budget pressures	orderly planning and budgeting of resources
4	Giving based on pledging certain amounts	Proportionate giving based on first fruits
5	Giving measured by mathematical averages	Giving measured by ministry and missions potential
6	Concern with both dollars and finding workers for the church	Abundant numbers of believers who demonstrate true discipleship
7	A maintenance method based on harvesting and fund-raising.	A missional system based on nurturing and education.

For the most part, church stewardship problems arise from giving that has been based on needs and budgets. These problems result in members giving 2-3% of their income, of what has been left over. The budget, instead of being used for a spending control, has been used as a guide for giving. The solution is to teach biblical principles of giving. Healthy congregations do exactly that, motivating members spiritually to give generous first fruits and tithes. Based on learned scriptural principles, they recognize the conflicting approaches between a maintenance, harvesting type of stewardship and a grace-filled, seed-planting type.

TRADITIONAL STEWARDSHIP BASED ON MAINTENANCE AND NEEDS	BIBLICAL STEWARDSHIP BASED ON GRACE AND EDUCATION
Members give **to** certain needs or to the church buget	members give **from** what God has given (through the church to God)
Individuals give their share of the budet	Individuals give share of their income
Importance placed on doing— what the individual member **does**	Importance placed on being— who the individual member **is** in Christ
Has an abundance of meetings	Displays abundance of ministry
Requests money for church's scarcity and poverty	Recognizes God's abundance and the multiple resources available in the church
Members acknowledge parts of life and their resources	Members acknowledge all of life and all of their resources
Grows budgets— gains money for the church	Grows Christians— gains people for God
Operates with leftovers	Operates by first fruits
Uses mirror or tunnel vision	Has world mission vision
Operates on a dull, failed system based on dismal statistics	Operates on a dynamic system based on grace

God's focus is not on an individual's share of the budget, but on His share of that individual's income. The task is not centered on how a few more dollars can be acquired in order to meet increased budget needs. The task is not to meet costs by fundraising, but to change giving habits. The concern is not about group financial results, but about individual commitments of a definite percentage dedicated to God. The concern is not with more dollars for the church, but about making more disciples.

Member giving has all too often been guided by budgets and legalistic appeals. These only deal with symptoms of the problem rather than with biblical principles. Pressure tactics, budget appeals, needs-centered programs, second and third offerings, sales, bazaars, raffles, and "Oktoberfests" are only too familiar in church fund-raising efforts. Unfortunately, they have been substituted for biblical giving. While churches have raised more money to maintain their minimum programs, they have failed to reach their financial potential based on the full resources God has placed into their hands.

The 21st century church culture has tended to change stewards into consumers. Many churches have treated members as donors rather than disciples. Twenty percent of its members give most of the gifts. New affluence is not congruous with the budget and small vision. These symptoms are exacerbated by crisis fundraising tactics and people being pressured for money. Church finances seem to be more about harvesting than seed-planting and nurturing. The truth is, the church does not have a harvesting or money problem, but one of seed-planting and nurturing. There has been little scriptural foundation laid for a stewardship based on grace and education.

Is the church willing to use the budget to empty the treasury rather than to make an appeal to fill it? Does it realize that the problem is one of "empty heads" (persons who lack a scriptural foundation and education), not of empty bank accounts?

PAUL'S STYLE—PRODUCTIVE SEED-PLANTING AND NURTURING OF BELIEVERS

Paul's primary principles for the stewardship of giving are found in 2 Corinthians, chapters 8 and 9. These biblical principles for funding the ministry and mission of the church are to be taught diligently to God's people. They need to be informed and motivated in order to be productive servants.

Principle 1: It is God's grace and power that make people productive and generous in giving (2 Corinthians 8:1-2). In this passage, Paul reveals how God showed His grace and kindness to believers in the churches in Macedonia. Though they were in extreme poverty, they were very generous in their giving. This kind of giving results from God's grace, not from anyone's own strength and ingenuity—or from fund-raising tactics.

Principle 2: Grace-filled people give offerings beyond their natural abilities and are eager to participate in the ministry of the gospel with their gifts (2 Corinthians 8:3-4). The Macedonian Christians were motivated by Christ's love and God's grace. They were so motivated that they begged Paul to let them participate in the offering for God's people in Jerusalem.

Principle 3: Christian giving begins with individuals giving of themselves to God and others, then extending generous offerings for the work of Christ's kingdom (2 Corinthians 8:5). The order is important: first giving self to God and others, and then giving gifts to God.

Principle 4: The stronger the faith, the greater the offerings (2 Corinthians 8:6-7). Good knowledge along with great faith and love increase the giving, but that is not all. It also inspires others "to participate in this work of God's kindness."

Principle 5: Giving for ministry is a test of the authenticity of love (2 Corinthians 8:8). Offerings are not to be given because of a command to give, but rather because it is an expression of love and sincerity. Genuine love will be shown in generous gifts.

Principle 6: The grace of Christ enriches each giver and is the power for giving (2 Corinthians 8:9). In taking on humanity and earthly poverty, Jesus made those who trust Him rich. He is the model for all giving. In a sense, Christ exchanged His riches for rags, but now takes our "rags for His riches."

Principle 7: God wants givers to finish what they have begun (2 Corinthians 8:10-11). Willingness to do ministry should be matched by ample gifts to finish the tasks. God wants His work fully completed through generous offerings.

Principle 8: God asks His people to give from what they have, not from what they do not have (2 Corinthians 8:12). When people say they do not have money to give, they should know that God does not expect them to give from what they do not have. He only asks for gifts from all they do have—their actual resources, income, investments, and whatever else He has given.

Principle 9: Generous giving comes full circle when one person's surplus fills another's needs and the second person's surplus fills the first's need (2 Corinthians 8:13-15). No matter which circumstance may present itself, each believer has the same call and responsibility to share his or her assets with others. Scripture gives this example: "Those who had gathered a lot didn't have too much, and those who gathered a little didn't have too little."

Principle 10: In order to represent the Church and bring glory to Christ, messengers or ambassadors are to be sent in order to prepare God's people to be generous (2 Corinthians 8:16-24). Paul sent Titus to the churches to encourage them to give willingly. In the same way, dedicated workers are to visit and encourage God's people in order to spur them on to generous giving.

Principle 11: Sharing testimonies and grace-inspired examples of generous giving are fully appropriate in the church (2 Corinthians 9:1-5). Paul commended the Macedonian Christians publicly (2 Corinthians 8:1-2) for one striking reason: God's grace makes people generous!

Many churches do not want to use testimonies because they are afraid that humans will be given the credit. But in not telling the good news, they are denying believers the blessings both of receiving the encouragement to give generously from others and of giving God the credit!

Principle 12: Sow a little, reap a little. Sow a lot, reap a lot (2 Corinthians 9:6). This is the same lesson learned from the farmer. Believers reap what they sow in respect to their giving. What God gives is given in His own time and in His own way—all by His grace. But the harvest is also given according to the measure sown.

Principle 13: God loves a cheerful giver (2 Corinthians 9:7). God outlines clear principles of giving. He also makes it clear that His grace supplies the power to be generous. Those who know God's principles and His power will not give small gifts. God loves those who love to give joyfully.

Principle 14: A giver can never outgive God (2 Corinthians 9:8-11). This scripture is loaded with promises of God's grace! Each believer is promised everything necessary for life. Just as God gives seed to the farmer, He also gives the Seed of His Word. He gives financial seed to the extent that He "will make you rich enough so that you can always be generous. Your generosity will produce thanksgiving to God..."

Principle 15: Generous giving blesses all of God's people and causes them to be grateful for what God has done (2 Corinthians 9:12-14). Those who are fearful of teaching biblical principles of giving need to consider Paul's words. Offerings given do not only serve the needs of God's people, but produce more and more prayers of thanksgiving to God. He receives glory! Giving is a genuine act of service which honors God as it spreads the Good News of Christ. Generous giving also results in deep affection from those who are blessed. These recipients will pray for those who gave out of the grace God has shown them.

Principle 16: True Christian giving is a response to God's incredible gift (2 Corinthians 9:15). "Words cannot describe" God's gracious gift—the gift of His Son, Jesus Christ, for the salvation of all. Decisions regarding giving, including the size of the gift, are to be settled at the foot of the cross and offered in thanksgiving to God.

FAITHFUL, GENEROUS BELIEVERS ARE LIKE TREES PLANTED BY WATER

As stated in Psalm 1, the person who delights in the teaching of the Lord and lives accordingly is "like a tree planted beside streams—a tree that produces fruit in season and whose leaves do not whither" (verse 3). A tree with good nutrition and water will have a healthy root system, a robust trunk, and flourishing branches bearing fruit. Green leaves and good fruit are the byproducts of a good root system, a supportive trunk, proper nourishment, sunlight, and ample water.

As a branch on Christ's vine, Christians are productive only due to a sturdy root system deeply grounded in the Word. This root system is strengthened as it is immersed in consistent godly teaching, counsel, and fellowship. It is built up through time alone in God's Word as well as with fellow believers. Believers are grafted into the vine or trunk, none other than Christ, the Savior. They are deeply rooted in the Word, by grace through faith in Jesus. They are "in Him" as He is in them. As branches grafted into Christ, their fruit is Christian witness and ministries of service. They are like trees planted next to living water. Their lives are productive and are a witness and praise to God.

Some weak believers remain closely associated with the evil culture of the world. "They have dug their own cisterns, broken cisterns that can't hold water" (Jeremiah 2:13). They are trying to sustain themselves in a self-imposed wilderness. They deceive themselves as they look at the Dead Sea, believing it will be refreshing. Meanwhile, they ignore "the fountain of life-giving water" that flows from God's Word. God invites all to be healthy trees and come to the waters, all to His glory.

The fruitfulness of all creation serves and praises God. He has not only created plants, animals, and people, but has also given them powers to be productive and bloom. God's unrestrained creation does not keep silent, but shouts with fruit and beauty to God who gives it strength. All together it joins with heartfelt joy to sing its Maker's praise.

Johann Mentzer gave voice to nature as it praises its Creator. In his hymn, "Oh, That I Had a Thousand Voices," believers are encouraged to join in that praise:

> You forest leaves so green and tender
> That dance for joy in summer air,
> You meadow grasses, bright and slender,
> You flow'rs so fragrant and so fair,
> You live to show God's praise alone,
> Join me to make His glory known.

> All creatures that have breath and motion,
> That throng the earth, the sea, the sky,
> Come, share with me my heart's devotion,
> Help me to sing God's praises high.

My utmost pow'rs can never quite
Declare the wonders of His might.

God's servant David broke out in resounding praise and adoration. "Give to the Lord the glory His name deserves." He wrote. "Bring an offering, and come before him. Worship the Lord in His holy splendor" (1 Chronicles 16:29). Disciples of Jesus Christ have a heart like David's, one that wants to sing highest praise to God. They echo Mentzer's thoughts, that they could not possibly declare all the wonders of God's might.

GOD'S BASIC PRINCIPLE OF THE GIVING OF FIRST FRUITS

James 1:18 reveals an important principle. Through the Seed of the Word, believers are the first fruits—the most important—of all God has created. God gave His first and only Son, who gave Himself for us. As a reminder that Christ comes first in believer's lives, God established the Old Testament practice that His people give of the first fruits of all the produce received from Him.

Before the time of Christ, the law required that the people bring God the first and best of all they reaped. Exodus 23 summarizes His command. "Celebrate the Festival of the Harvest with the first produce harvested from whatever you plant in your field…You must bring the best of the first produce harvested from your soil to the house of the Lord your God" (Exodus 23:16, 19). This is not a fundraising plea, but rather a principle for seed-planters. It is a precept for persons who have experienced the increase which God has given in their partnership with Him.

The book of Proverbs further expounds upon this principle and promise of giving God the first and the best. "Honor the Lord with your wealth and with the first and best part of all your income. Then your barns will be full and your vats will overflow with fresh wine" (Proverbs 3:9-10).

Before Christ, God's people were required to bring one tenth of all that they received from God before using any of their increase. The prophet Malachi clearly distinguishes between God's pleasure over those who give generously and His displeasure over those who deprive Him of tithes and offerings. "Can a person cheat God? Yet, you are cheating me! But you ask, 'How are we cheating you?' When you don't bring a tenth of your income and other contributions. So a curse is on you because the whole nation is cheating me! Bring one-tenth of your income into the storehouse so that there may be food in my house. Test me in this way…See if I won't open the windows of heaven for you and flood you with blessings…All nations will call you blessed because you will be a delightful land" (Malachi 3:8-10, 12).

Believers, first of all, give offerings to God from their income. There are biblical and practical reasons they do so.

1. God provides all that is needed from His resources. Everything God's people own is His. He gave them everything they have. God is the gracious Giver. "Every creature in the forest, even the cattle on a thousand hills, is mine. I know every bird in the mountains. Everything that moves in the field is mine. If I were hungry, I would not tell you, because the world and all that it contains are mine…Bring your thanks to God as a sacrifice, and keep your vows to the Most High" (Psalm 50:10-12, 14).

In any earthly estimation, as well as in the eyes of the law, Christians appear to "own" what they have. But in God's eyes, they are only managers. Possessions are theirs in relation to other people, not in reference to God. God gives them various resources, but He can take them away in a multitude of ways. Believers call their possessions "theirs" only in relation to what is "His." All possessions are God's.

2. God offers contentment and peace in financial matters. Paul makes this clear. "A godly life brings huge profits to people who are content with what they have. We didn't bring anything into the world, and we can't take anything out of it. As long as we have food and clothes, we should be satisfied. But people who want to get rich keep falling into temptation. They are trapped by many stupid and harmful desires which drown them in destruction and ruin. Certainly, the love of money is the root of all kinds of evil. Some people who have set their hearts on getting rich have wandered away from the Christian faith and have caused themselves a lot of grief. But you, man of God, must avoid these things. Pursue what God approves of: a godly life, faith, love, endurance, and gentleness" (1 Timothy 6:6-11).

3. God promises to take care of all basic needs and guide His people in financial decisions. He works graciously "to give an inheritance to those who love Me and to fill their treasuries" (Proverbs 8:21). What a promise!

4. God uses what believers give to strengthen the work and outreach of His Church. This is seen so clearly in 2 Corinthians 8 and 9. Simply stated, Christian stewardship blesses God's people and His Church. "Whatever you plant is what you'll harvest. If you plant in the soil of your corrupt nature, you will harvest destruction. But if you plant in the soil of your spiritual nature, you will harvest everlasting life. We can't allow ourselves to get tired of living the right way. Certainly, each of us will receive everlasting life at the proper time, if we don't give up. Whenever we have the opportunity, we have to do what is good for everyone, especially for the family of believers" (Galatians 6:7-10). According to Paul, the Christian life is all about planting and productivity.

5. *God will take what is given and multiply it for His purposes.* Among a gathered people, God took what was given, five loaves of barley bread and two small fish, and multiplied them to supply what was needed (John 6:5-14). God supplied all that the widow needed at Zarephath. "This is what the Lord God of Israel says: Until the Lord sends rain on the land, the jar of flour will never be empty and the jug will always contain oil" (1 Kings 17: 14). God allows this to happen in present-day ministry, to His glory!

6. *God does not require us to be full of resources, but to be full of faith.* Paul makes it clear in 1 Corinthians 4:2 that "managers are required to be trustworthy." He was only echoing what Jesus had said repeatedly. God's people are to be faithful with the little or much that God has given them. Gifts are measured by faith, not by amounts. To faithfully use what has been so graciously given is all that God asks.

JESUS EMPHASIZED THE PRIORITY PRINCIPLE TO "PUT GOD FIRST"

In His Sermon on the Mount, Jesus announced the priority principle for the handling of possessions, including any kind of financial assets and income. He taught the "God first" principle. "But first, be concerned about His [heavenly Father's] kingdom and what has His approval. Then all these things will be provided for you" (Matthew 6:33). The principle is simple: When what has been given to God is the first part, He is honored. When the first fruits are given before any food, clothing, homes, cars, and all resources are enjoyed, He willingly provides what is needed. The context of Jesus' teaching makes a series of lessons very clear (Matthew 6:19-24).

1. "Stop storing up treasures for yourselves on earth, where moths and rust destroy and thieves break in and steal. Instead, store up treasures for yourselves in heaven where moths and rust don't destroy and thieves don't break in and steal" (verses 19-20). Some persons may lose their entire fortune, but those who put God first in their giving will never lose what they have given to God. It can never be destroyed or lost, but will be stored up in heaven for the good of Christ's kingdom.

2. "Your heart will be where your treasure is" (verse 21). A person's heart will be set on whatever he or she treasures in life, whether earthly possessions or Christ. Jesus says that it cannot be a divided heart. "No one can serve two masters. He will hate the first master and love the second, or he will be devoted to the first and despise the second. You cannot serve God and wealth" (verse 24). Either Christ or temporal issues will control an individual. Jesus emphasized His Father's desire that His people have an undivided heart. "Love the Lord your God with all your heart, with all your soul, and with all your mind" (Deuteronomy 6:4 and Matthew 22:37).

The crucial question: Who is number one? There is a great civil war going on inside every Christian. It is the war between the forces of God and the forces of evil. The indwelling Christ within a believer creates a strong pull to God. The sinful nature within creates a strong pull to things of the world. This great struggle was overcome by the crucifixion and resurrection of our Lord and Savior Jesus Christ. He alone is to control us. It is He who asks us to seek God first. We cannot serve Him and earthly things at the same time. What one chooses determines preeminence, one's focus in life. There is no doubt left regarding the issue. Jesus says there is no such thing as half-heartedness or double-mindedness. A person's heart will be where his treasure lies.

3. Life must be lived with eyes of faith! "The eye is the lamp of the body…But if your eye is evil, your whole body will be full of darkness. If the light in you is darkness, how dark it will be!" Verses 22-23 seem to get off the subject of management of riches and possessions, but Jesus' entire teaching in this section (verses 19-24) is centered on the issue of faith. Jesus here is speaking about the "eye of faith." In verse 30, He indicates that His hearers had little faith. He seems to be saying something like this: "If a person's eye of faith is weak or bad, his life will be full of doubt and indecision. He won't be able to understand what he is facing. What's more, if you have no faith, life and possessions will make no sense whatsoever." Believers must have the eyes of <u>faith</u>.

4. "…Stop worrying about what you will eat, drink, or wear. Isn't life more than food and the body more than clothes" (verse 25). Jesus' teaching in verses 25–32 tells His disciples to stop worrying, and tells how. He gives the answer to the person who asks, "Well, we need to live, don't we? We need to buy food and clothes in order to exist, don't we?" In Jesus' economy, the bigger question is, "For what do you live?" What are true necessities for daily living? How do we keep material wants and desires in proper perspective?

Jesus is speaking about food and clothing—the essentials of bodily existence. He does not say that believers should not think about earthly things or plan carefully. Rather, He says that His people should not have worldly cares. They should not have to worry about acquiring these basic needs.

The key question here is whether life is more important than food, and the body more important than clothes. Jesus says that believers should be more concerned about God's purpose and meaning for their lives than what they put into their mouths. How they use their bodies is far more important than what they drape over them. Christ's representatives on earth need to concentrate on living their lives and using their bodies purposefully, not worrying about where they will get food and clothes. There are many biblical warnings concerning preoccupation with the pursuit of physical desires, comforts, and material things. The dangers of being absorbed with these things are explicit and numerous.

The present culture causes humans to fall prey to the false rewards of materialism. People spend prodigally. They dispense an abundance of God's gifts on luxury items, many of them different models of the same item. A world driven by sports mania, frivolity, feasting, smoking, seems to shout out, "Serve me! Amuse me! Pamper me! I want what I want, and I want it now!"

In the parable of the sower, the cares of the world and the delight in riches are thorns that choke out the Seed of the Word (Matthew 13:22). When the rich man stocks up worldly goods, Jesus labels him a fool for "laying out treasures on earth" while he was not "rich with God" (Luke 12:21, 33). Modern worries, like the examples in Jesus' parables, do not match the ways of God's kingdom.

5. "Look at the birds. They don't plant, harvest, or gather the harvest into barns. Yet, your heavenly Father feeds them. Aren't you worth more than they?" (verse 26). Birds must wait for plants and trees to grow leaves and fruit. Not so with God's people! They are assured of a heavenly Father who will graciously provide all they need. Yet sadly, many do not realize that they are much better off than the birds!

Martin Luther succinctly exposed that kind of short sightedness. "Now is it not a crying shame that we cannot trust our bellies to God without concern and greed? If anyone has a reason for being concerned it is the little birds…Yet the bird is happier in the woods than cooped up in a cage." Luther's words bare the awesome fact that the bird in a cage must rely on a human to supply its food, while a bird in the woods is supplied its sustenance by nature. God's people are children of the heavenly Father!

6. "Don't worry," Jesus says pointedly. "Can any of you add a single hour to your life by worrying?" (verse 27). Humans are very limited in their ability to add or subtract from the life span that God has given. Worry will not change one moment for the better. Yes, blessings of nutrition and medicine make a difference. But Jesus says it is impossible to add one or ten years to anyone's life by worrying. God has chosen each person's cradle, and He has chosen each grave. Should not believers' lives be fully placed in His hands from birth to death?

7. The heavenly Father will clothe His people. "And why worry about clothes? Notice how the flowers grow in the field. They never work or spin yarn for clothes. But I say that not even Solomon in all his majesty was dressed like one of these flowers. That's the way God clothes the grass in the fields. Today it's alive and tomorrow it's thrown into an incinerator. So how much more will He clothe you people who have so little faith?" (verses 28-30).

Think of how God dresses and sustains flowers even in a desert or jungle where no human being will ever view them. They explode with brilliant color and splendor! If God clothes them without human help, will He not make necessary garments available? Martin Luther believed, in this passage, that Jesus "is talking satirically, in order to describe how abominable our unbelief is...each individual flower is a witness against us to condemn our unbelief." Jesus most certainly is targeting worry and doubt! He asks, "So how much more will He clothe you people who have so little faith?" Faith that doubts is not faith at all! Faith and trust in an all-powerful loving God drive out any semblance of fear or worry.

8. "Don't ever worry and say, 'What are we going to eat?' or 'What are we going to drink?' or 'What are we going to wear?' Everyone is concerned about these things, and your heavenly Father certainly knows you need all of them" (verses 31-32). At this point, it is tempting to say, "Just a minute! Please don't insult my intelligence! You said the same thing six verses back. I remember it very well!" Why would Jesus repeat this same thought here? Simply because God knows how human and frail and worrisome His people are. God seems to be pleading, "I am your Creator and Provider. Therefore, don't take things into your own hands by worrying! Trust me!"

The reminder is clear: "Your heavenly Father certainly knows you need all of them." Believers have higher goals and commitments than those who doubt God. Such anxiety is not appropriate in the lives of those who know and experience God's love and care daily. The call is to believe God!

9. In his sermon, Jesus had reviewed human concerns that demonstrate doubt of God's providence and love. At His conclusion, He provided the priority principle, "God first," in the use of resources. He gives the answer to the question, "*Who* comes first?" Jesus says, "But first, be concerned about His kingdom and what has His approval. Then all these things will be provided for you" (verse 33).

Jesus outlines an order of priority for the spending of money: (1) God's glory, (2) personal needs and the needs of others. He says, "Never have any other god" (Exodus 20:3). In Matthew 22:37-39 Jesus is saying, "Love God with your whole self…seek the good of others as you love yourself, in the way He loves you." Verse 33 of the Sermon on the Mount shows that believers are to be concerned first about God's kingdom. It is in that kingdom that all Christians "die to self" through the use of their time, abilities and money. They have been forgiven and made right with God. They are indwelt by the Holy Spirit. They now, by the working of that same Spirit, seek to live in this righteousness. This is the New Testament principle of life in Christ.

Christians are to live lives that have God's approval. "Don't work for food that spoils. Instead, work for the food that lasts into eternal life" (John 6:27). Seeking God before all else not only has God's stamp of approval, but also His promise. "Then all these things [food, drink, clothes]," Jesus says, "will be provided for you" (verse 33). Jesus' sermon indicates that "these things" are not luxuries, but essentials for life. The necessities of life will be given by a most gracious God in His own way and in His own time.

Earthly circumstances are fully in the hands of God. Some persons seek certain worldly goods but never get them, while others acquire the goods they seek, but are only able to enjoy them for a short while. Others discover that their ability to enjoy is gone. Paul's writings clearly demonstrate the principle of "God first." Believers are to turn first to Christ, putting to death their carnal and fleshly desires. They are to seek the things of God and be filled with the Holy Spirit.

In this world, many fail due to tragically misplaced priorities. They transpose Matthew 6:33 as they seek first "all these things" (food, drink, clothes), hoping the kingdom of God will be theirs as well. Jesus' "kingdom first" priority principle had boldly answered the question, "*Who* comes first?"

Jesus did not simply say, "Don't worry!" He said, "*First*, be concerned about God's kingdom and what has His approval…. *Then* all these things will be provided for you." The heavenly Father knows what those needs are and will provide them in His own way and timing. Christians have nothing to worry about! The principle is simple. Before they seek anything else, they must seek after the kingdom of God and the good of their spiritual lives.

Paul recorded several examples of the "kingdom first" priority principle. The believers in Macedonia practiced it faithfully. "First, they gave themselves to the Lord and to us, since this was God's will" (2 Corinthians 8:5). Paul had also told the Corinthian Christians, "Every Sunday each of you should set aside some of your money…" (1 Corinthians 16:2). Christians were to have the assurance that if they gave to God first, they would not need to worry about earthly needs.

The Christian life is designed to be lived as a dedication of all time, abilities, and money to the glory of God. Believers are to freely give them as a tribute to the heavenly Father who created them and to the Lord Jesus who redeemed them. This is the commitment to Christ's priority principle to "put God first."

Martin Luther made some helpful observations. No matter what circumstances may be, he said, "God will not let our earthly situation make a liar out of Him. Just believe!" Can God's promises be believed or not? Pointedly, are believers willing to simply believe God? When it comes to faith, life is designed to be a constant witness to our Lord Jesus Christ! In life and faith, their life's intent is to demonstrate victory by the power of the Holy Spirit. This means simply seek God first! In their life of faith, they will live sensibly and practice good management of their physical goods. The mandate is to seek God first! In their life of faith, Christians will seek first the kingdom of God, knowing that anything they need will be provided for them!

Henry Drummond gives a sharp reminder for adopting correct priorities. "Above all else," he writes, "do not touch Christianity unless you are willing to seek God first. I promise you a miserable existence if you seek Him second." Many people are miserable because they are seeking God second, not first—despite ever-increasing incomes. Putting God first is an act of faith. It is first of all spiritual, then material and physical. The "God first" principle is the key He gives for happiness, security, and success. It is not a bargain the steward makes with God, for God makes no deals. It is God's provision of joy, security, and success—a gift of His grace.

Scripture is the basis for some strong considerations for believers regarding their giving. First, the New Testament under grace nowhere suggests that Christians should give less than a tenth or a tithe of their income. It is important for everyone to know that the tithe is not the full measure of their response to God. He is also very concerned about the nine-tenths a person keeps. Jesus' own standard, in fact, was always higher than the law or the tithe, never lower. It is also important that Christians know, however, that scripture never suggests they should either tithe from a sense of legal obligation or give with the expectation of financial gain.

The most important consideration of all, though, is that of motivation. The gift must be given with a whole, undivided heart, one of love toward God and His kingdom. In fact, love does not set mathematical standards, nor does it fix certain rates or limits to giving. Tithing is a commendable practice, but God's grace empowers His people to give by faith beyond the tenth. Christian love puts God first.

THE FIRST, BIG OFFERING IS A REPENTANT HEART

In His Sermon on the Mount, Jesus offered some strong advice. It is a surprising priority principle, one that unfortunately is not proclaimed in many churches or known by most members. "So if you are offering your gift at the altar and remember there that another believer has something against you, leave your gift at the altar. First go away and make peace with that person. Then come back and offer your gift" (Matthew 5:23-24). What is the priority? God's people are to be reconciled with repentant hearts, before bringing a financial gift. God wants reconciliation, not money.

Repentant hearts turn from self-centeredness and sinful behavior to God. They recognize that they have placed self first, ahead of the things of God. The repentance Jesus spoke of is characterized by a broken spirit and produces obedience, loyalty to God, and love of God and others. Various scripture messages propose the same kind of incredible request of God's people:

1. *A broken spirit*—In Psalm 51, David clearly recognized what pleased God. "You are not happy with any sacrifice. Otherwise, I would offer one to you. You are not pleased with burnt offerings. The sacrifice pleasing to God is a broken spirit. O God, you do not despise a broken and sorrowful heart. Favor Zion with your goodness…then you will be pleased with sacrifices offered in the right spirit…" (Psalm 51: 16-19). Even though God had commanded His people to make sacrifices and

offerings, He indicated that he does not want them unconditionally. What first does He require? Not financial gifts. He wants the first, big offering. A broken, repentant heart.

2. *Obedience*—God's Word spoken through Samuel was just as surprising. "Is the Lord as delighted with burnt offerings and sacrifices as He would be with your obedience? To follow instructions is better than to sacrifice. To obey is better than sacrificing the fat of rams" (1 Samuel 15:22). What is the priority? Obedience—following the instructions God had given—not sacrifices and offerings.

The message God gave through the prophet Isaiah about giving to God came as a bombshell. "What do your many animal sacrifices mean to me? I've had enough of your burnt offerings of rams and enough fat from your fattened calves. I'm not pleased with the blood of bulls, lambs or male goats. When you appear in my presence, who asked you to trample on my courtyards? Don't bring any more worthless grain offerings. Your incense is disgusting to me…I can't stand your evil assemblies…So when you stretch out your hands in prayer, I will turn my eyes away from you…If you are willing and obedient, you will eat the best from the land. But if you refuse and rebel, you will be destroyed by swords" (Isaiah 1:11-13, 15, 19-20). What is the priority God wants? He wants His people to be willing and obedient. He does not want them to bring meaningless sacrifices and offerings.

3. *Loyalty*—Another amazing message was given through Hosea. "I want your loyalty, not your sacrifices. I want you to know me, not to give me burnt offerings" (Hosea 6:6). What is the first, big gift? Loyalty to God. It is knowing Him and having a living relationship with Jesus Christ, not giving sacrifices and offerings.

4. *Love*—Jesus summarized these priority teachings in Mark 12:30-33, "'Love the Lord your God with all your heart, with all your soul, with all your mind, and with all your strength,'" He said. "The second most important commandment is this: 'Love your neighbor as you love yourself.' No other commandment is greater than these." A scribe said to Jesus, "Teacher, that was well said! You've told the truth that there is only one God and no other besides Him! To love Him with all your heart, with all your understanding, with all your strength, and to love your neighbor as you love yourself is more important than all the burnt offerings and sacrifices."

What is the priority, according to Jesus? His people are to love God with all their heart, understanding, and strength, and then to love their neighbor as themselves. The simple, consistent stewardship priority in scripture is that of giving the first, big love offering. The giver is to give first of self, complete with a whole, repentant, and forgiven heart.

But can Christians today realistically be expected to bring repentant hearts and lives to the altar before they give their offerings? It seems too rigid and demanding. For most, it would seem to be too drastic a change in giving habits.

Typical church giving and fund-raising practices clearly conflict with God's Word. Church members often bring offerings without being reconciled with each other. They come without repentant hearts. They come in a spirit of disobedience before God, not following His will. But how can God's people be introduced to the principle that the first, big stewardship offering is the repentant heart?

Great benefits await the pastor and spiritual leaders of the church who communicate the "God first" principle orally and in writing. Its basis in scripture can be delivered in sermons and studied in Bible classes. A special gathering can be scheduled to direct congregation members away from the focus on budgets and financial needs, while inspiring them in "God first" principles. This type of gathering aims to begin setting believers' hearts and minds on Christ as top priority in financial matters.

Church leaders can make oral and written announcements to the members such as the following: "Your pastor and spiritual leaders want to offer an apology for contributing toward a misunderstanding concerning members' giving and financial stewardship for the ministries of our church. In the past few months, we have been studying God's Word in the area of giving and finances. We believe that churches everywhere, including ours, have given members the impression that the church needs people's money in order to maintain God's work. We believe members were led to believe it is their duty to give, regardless of their relationship with God.

"As we studied several key passages from the Bible, we were convicted to share clearly what scripture says. First, God is interested in the spiritual condition of His people. He desires that Jesus is first in their lives, that their first, big offering is not money, but a repentant heart. 'So if you are offering your gift at the altar and remember there that another believer has something against you, leave your gift at the alter. First go away and make peace with that person. Then come back and offer your gift' (Matthew 5:23-24). He wants them to make certain they are reconciled with everyone in their personal network. Several scriptures have been especially meaningful to us in our study. (Name here the previous scriptures and summarize their messages.)

"We want to encourage you personally to think of the offerings you give to God within a new framework. First, are you right with God? Have you given your heart fully to God in repentance and forgiveness? When you are right with God and put Christ first, you are ready to bring generous first fruit offerings.

"We, your pastor and spiritual leaders, want to confess our part in contributing toward this misunderstanding concerning your giving and financial stewardship. From this point on, the stewardship approach of our congregation will not be fund-raising, but people-raising. It is our commitment to regularly gather together to hear and study the Word of God, for our spiritual growth, to be healthy Christians. We commit to be faithful witnesses of the saving gospel. We commit to be faithful servants of Christ who express their faith visibly through offerings that demonstrate heartfelt gratitude for the great gifts that God has given.

"Our priority as leaders of this congregation is that each person is closely connected with this body and has a living relationship with God in Christ Jesus. We desire that, by His grace, you make service, witnessing, and giving a priority in your life as you move forward in that relationship. In Matthew 6:33, Jesus says that His people are to seek Him and the things of His kingdom even before food and clothes. We pray that from this point on, the stewardship and giving efforts in this church will be done in God's way, not our own. Please join us in our prayer. Join us as we look forward to what God does as we seek Him, putting His kingdom first!"

True stewardship is honoring God's Word and pursuing His priorities. True stewardship is first giving self to God—in repentance and forgiveness—and only then bringing offerings by the strength He gives. By doing God's work in God's way, His church will experience miracles that enable them to use generous gifts to aggressively perform the ministry of the Word.

THREE STEPS FOR SUCCESSFUL FUND-RAISING AND STEWARDSHIP GIVING

Three steps are necessary for success in stewardship giving, only by the power of the Holy Spirit: (1) Law-and-Gospel-oriented messages, (2) sufficient information, and (3) a good system.

1. *Law-and-Gospel-Oriented Messages*—It would be a grave mistake to fail to undergird stewardship messages with a clear presentation of law and gospel. The war between the old nature and the new nature is at fever pitch when believers are faced with stewardship and giving responsibilities. Stewardship failures are instigated by the human condition. The sinful nature promotes stewardship failures as well by the temptation and deceit of the devil. The only cure for spiritual sluggishness and stubbornness in any area, including stewardship delinquencies, is first to expose them to God's law. This task is not one of showing failure to meet church budgets (merely a human evaluation of human failures). The issue here is one of failure to obey God's Word.

An example of this proper application of law is expressed in the first chapter of Haggai. In these times, God was displeased that some of His people were living in luxurious homes while His temple was in ruins. They were not concerned about the Lord's work. They began to experience crop failure and inflation. God said they sustained these consequences because their only concern was for their own good. They were ignoring His temple and the Lord's work. Was God cold and heartless in doing this? Not at all. They were destroying themselves due to their disregard of the very God who had created them and all of their possessions. They had failed to listen to His Word, the Word that had directed them to give Him their tithes and offerings in worship of Him. When God applied His law, holding back their income, He finally got their attention. In His grace, God gave them the opportunity to repent, experience forgiveness, and rebuild their relationship with Him.

In Malachi 1, the law was used to confront God's disobedient people when they withheld the offerings He had required. At this time the priests were also guilty. God told them, "A son honors his father, and a servant honors his master. So if I am a Father, where is my honor? If I am a master, where is my respect? You priests despise my name. But you ask 'How have we despised your name?' You offer contaminated food on my altar. But you ask 'Then how have we contaminated you?' When you say that the Lord's table may be despised. When you bring a blind animal to sacrifice, isn't that wrong? When you bring a lame or a sick animal, isn't that wrong? Try offering it to your governor. Would he accept it from you? Would he welcome you?" (Malachi 1:6-8).

God had required the first fruits and the best, but the priests allowed the people to bring leftovers, the sick and the crippled. Significantly, God told the priests that they should have shut the doors of the temple and refused people entrance because of their leftover offerings. This was not cruelty on God's part, for He wanted to provide an opportunity for a quick awakening. He was displeased with their worship. God told them, "From the nations where the sun rises to the nations where the sun sets, My name will be great. Incense and pure offerings will be offered everywhere in My name, because My name will be great among the nations…but you dishonor it when you say that the Lord's table may be contaminated and that its food may be despised" (verses 11-12).

God's solution to this problem was forgiveness and the kind of repentance that obeys Him and serves Him with tithes and offerings. God's message was: "Bring one-tenth of your income into the storehouse so that there may be food in My house. Test Me in this way…all nations will call you blessed because you will be a delightful land…" (Malachi 3:10, 12). The same is true today. The Gospel is not only a power unto salvation to everyone who believes, but also the power unto sanctification—the offering of self and substance to the Lord. This chapter is filled with Gospel selections that reveal that God's love is the only motivation and power to overcome our failure to obey God's law.

2. *Information*—People give as they know and believe, not as they are able. The truth is, most people do not have adequate knowledge of the biblical principles of giving. They are not aware of the scriptural teachings of generous first fruits. The stewardship task is to teach giving-truths to increase knowledge, while the Holy Spirit increases belief.

Instead of taking time to deal with the real problem—lack of stewardship knowledge—leaders often focus on the immediate financial needs of the church. They unfortunately take shortcuts and use fund-raising pressure tactics. But clever fund-raising approaches are not the answer. Promotional campaigns which tell about ministries to support can never replace careful teaching. These only make church members donors instead of disciples.

An important part of the church's mission is to transform believers from donors into authentic disciples. Fully devoted followers of Christ understand that giving is one of the primary steps to maturity of faith. Believers are to know that it is a part of their Christian lifestyle.

Stewardship information should provide solid biblical teachings, not just a series of inspirational stories or exhortations. Appeals to give for ministries, no matter how inspiring or convincing, are not a substitute for scriptural information that teaches God's principles of giving. Information is meat, while inspiration and exhortations are adrenaline. Meat gets into the sinews of the body, while adrenaline only stimulates for the moment.

Each message on the stewardship of giving needs to include information on correct giving principles. Christians are to (1) give to God first, (2) give a specific proportion or percentage that has been decided beforehand, (3) give a generous percentage, trying to exceed the 10 percent standard, (4) ask God for a strong faith, the kind that sets the proportion according to His priorities, and (5) ask God for the grace (or gift) of giving (2 Corinthians 8:1-2), since this is a gift God wants to give.

3. *A System*—There are three requisites for a successful system in stewardship and Christian giving: (a) a personal commitment, (b) an aggressive pastoral and lay leadership, and (c) a definable program.

a. *Commitment*—Christ explained his expectations of commitment in His parable about two sons (Matthew 21:28-31). He focused on the response of the two sons when they were requested to "work in the vineyard today." The first son apparently became angry and said he would not go. He later repented, changed his mind, and went to do the work. The second son told the father that he would go, but never went. When Jesus asked which of the two did the will of the father, the people answered, "The first."

Jesus then compared the people with the second son. He had talked a big game, but failed to obey and do the promised action. Jesus said that thieves and prostitutes would go into the kingdom of God before this kind of people did. This is a very serious indictment for this reason: there are many Christians who attend church regularly and make a general commitment, but they do not act or obey. Tragically, such persons face severe condemnation.

There is a third kind of son, not in the parable, who says he will go, and he goes. Christians should be challenged to be the third son by God's grace. If they choose to be like the first or second son, the gospel of forgiveness will be shared with them for them to change and go. They may get angry at the stewardship message or challenge it, as did the second son, but after reflecting on the truth that their Savior is asking them to work in the vineyard today, they may repent, change their mind, and do as they have been asked. It is vital that every Christian makes a clear commitment regarding the giving of a generous percentage of their income for God and follow through with it.

b. *Aggressive Pastoral and Lay Leadership*—Effective giving programs require an active partnership between the pastor and lay leaders. Both must accept responsibility and hold themselves accountable to perform this stewardship ministry according to God's call in His Word. If either pastor or lay leaders fail to exert strong influence and bold direction, it will be difficult to mobilize the entire membership. It will be difficult to succeed in nurturing God's field for productive giving.

God's high calling for Christian leaders is to nurture the faith and to challenge members of congregations to express that faith generously in bountiful giving. Scripture commends leaders for providing a stewardship ministry to God's people as a significant part of their spiritual ministry. As examples of this type of stewardship leader are reviewed in the Old and New Testaments, it can be seen that effective Christian leaders help people discover life as God intended. The God of the Bible yearns for believers to be active and real in their lives by providing gifts for the ministry of the Word.

Because everything written in the past was written to instruct believers (Romans 15:4), scripture is used to encourage pastors and lay leaders to plant seeds. It can be used to instruct God's people, planting in their minds stewardship seeds and providing proper nutrition, the kind that promotes generous giving. While technically some of these examples might be viewed as fund-raising activities, we can readily see that they were events of people-raising—calling God's people back to expressing their faith in action in financial matters.

(1) *Jesus' Teachings and Leadership*—the teaching of His parables that deal with the value and handling of money. Jesus showed strong leadership as He taught the "God first" principle (Matthew 6:33). His Matthew 5:23-24 teaching asks believers to be reconciled to others before they bring their offering to the altar. Jesus' own example of leadership reveals that the stewardship of giving is first of all spiritual—that only a healthy tree can bear bountiful fruit.

(2) *Paul's Example for Stewardship Ministry*—In 1 Corinthians 16:1-3, Paul's leadership in his letter not only encouraged the churches in Galatia, but also the church in Corinth to set aside money every Sunday for a gift to be sent to the church in Jerusalem. Paul's message in 2 Corinthians 8 and 9 is an exceptional grace message as a stewardship leader, one that gives instruction for generous and joyful giving.

(3) *The Apostles' Collections*—The apostles collected and gave money to those who needed it. Under their leadership, the believers showed amazing generosity. God's grace not only caused them to share the gospel with great power, but also with incredibly generous gifts to those in need (Acts 4:32-35).

(4) *Ezra's Freewill Offerings*—Ezra encouraged freewill offerings. The heads of families gave freewill offerings to help rebuild God's temple in Jerusalem (Ezra 2:68-69). The king sent Ezra a letter asking him to go to Jerusalem to evaluate the situation on the basis of God's teachings. Money given by the leaders was to be taken to buy bulls, rams, lambs, grain, and wine for the temple altar (7:11-23).

(5) *Nehemiah's Stewardship Program*—Nehemiah led God's people in a comprehensive stewardship program. He began his program with a prayer, praising God for showing mercy and keeping His promises despite the sins and wrongs done against Him by His people. He prayed for success, by God's great power (Nehemiah 1:4-11). Nehemiah wrote the king a letter requesting wood for the gate near the temple (2:7-8). He assessed the need (2:11-15). He conducted a leaders' meeting resulting in a commitment to "rebuild the wall" (2:16-18). He enlisted volunteers (3:4ff). He called a leaders' meeting to deal with a problem (5:7). Heads of families provided gifts for the temple (7:70). The leaders and people made a binding written agreement to follow God's commandments and to give generously, saying, "We won't neglect our God's temple" (9:38-10:1-39). Because of God's awesome goodness, the people rejoiced and gave many offerings and sacrifices, so much that "the sound of rejoicing in Jerusalem could be heard from far away" (12:43). When Nehemiah found that some had neglected to bring gifts for God's temple, he reprimanded the leaders. The people then brought "a tenth of all the grains harvested, new wine, and olive oil to the storerooms" and some were appointed to be in charge of the storerooms (13:10-13).

(6) *David's Vision Given to the People*— David was the one who led God's people to set their heart on building the temple and to give generously. He called a meeting of all the leaders in Jerusalem and told them, "I set my heart on building the temple." He asked his son Solomon to "serve the Lord wholeheartedly and willingly" (1 Chronicles 28:2,9). Then David said, "With all my might I gathered the materials for the temple of my God...I have a personal treasury of gold and silver that I am giving to my God's temple in addition to everything else I gathered..." (29:2-3). The leaders gave generously (29:6). The people were overjoyed that the leaders had given so generously and wholeheartedly to the Lord (29:9). David prayed, "I've been overjoyed to see Your people here offering so willingly to You...Keep their hearts directed towards You" (29:17-18).

David praised the Lord with a great doxology while the whole assembly watched. "May You be praised, Lord God of Israel, our Father forever and ever. Greatness, power, splendor, glory, and majesty are Yours, Lord, because everything in heaven and on earth is Yours. The kingdom is Yours, Lord, and You are honored as head of all things. Riches and honor are in front of You. You rule everything. You hold power and strength in Your hands, and You can make anyone great and strong. Our God, we thank You and praise Your wonderful name. But who am I and who are my people that You enable us to give so generously? Everything comes from You. We give You only what has come from Your hands" (29:10-15). Then David said to the whole assembly, "Praise the Lord Your God!" So the whole assembly praised the Lord God of their ancestors and knelt in front of the Lord and the king (29:20).

These six biblical accounts reveal how vital aggressive leadership is to effective stewardship of giving. Faithful leaders will use various forums to instruct God's people in the stewardship of giving for gospel ministries. Missional church leaders that have planted and cultivated stewardship seeds will not pick stewardship fruit by fundraising practices. These leaders, who have been planting seeds and nurturing them, will rather challenge God's people to express their faith in generous offerings, as did God's leaders many centuries ago.

c. *Definable Effective Program*—Successful congregations vary their programs and methods, but whatever approach they use, they reach all members with an organized biblical message. They may use personal member contacts, group discussion meetings, or a variety of other methods, but they always execute their plan effectively so all members are reached with the message. Recalling farmer Jim in his commitment to reach and care for every acre and every plant, church leaders will adopt a "guidance system" that will reach every member, not overlooking anyone.

Sound biblical messages must be combined with effective methods. Pious phrases and blind faith will not administer or finance the kingdom. Some pastors and leaders dismiss structured programs and offer no effective activity to accomplish what needs to be done. Leaders are responsible for any such organizational vacuum. The problem is the failure to understand the function of the activity to be pursued. These congregations fail to have stewardship committees and choose not to pursue other effective programs. The fact is, the Creator God is a God of order and method.

A Detroit layman expressed the importance of effective methods: "For generations, Satan has sold us on the idea that Christian sacrificial giving dare only be dealt with in abstract terms. Because many people are inclined to take offense at the subject, we believe we dare not confront one another. Personally, I thank God that I have been confronted with some of these messages.

"I was down there in the lower two thirds of the congregation, among the poor givers," he said. "I had heard the church expounding upon its needs in eloquent form for 30 years. I figured I was doing all or more than my share. Somehow the message never got through to me—nor to most of my fellow members. But now, for the first time in my life I have learned the joy of proportionate giving."

Method is vital in the transmission of a lively stewardship and giving message. Paul believed in going beyond a general proclamation of the stewardship message. He stated the case of Christian giving to the Corinthians in classic terms. Yet he sent men out to make sure that the people were properly cultivated and prepared (2 Corinthians 9:3)—a specific effort at confrontation.

Leaders must speak the truth to the people boldly. They must do this with consistent, continuous education in stewardship principles. When stewards are effectively taught, the resources will be available to do the work of Christ's Church.

From 1 Corinthians 3:9, it is clear that each Christian is a field under God's cultivation, as is each Christian congregation. Christians and congregations, however, are not finished products. They are not like a field whose grain has fully ripened and is ready for harvest. They need cultivators, planters, and waterers to bring programs of education, stewardship and evangelism.

Life is made of seasons of sowing and growing. The whole work of the church is the story of the sower who went to sow. Pastors, teachers, and leaders are called to give a full measure of devotion to the work. But they must go the whole way, from seedtime to harvest! The old nature would like to have half-seasons or jump from sowing to harvest, without cultivating. But there is just no place for workers who watch the clock or who want half a season so that they can lounge on "Florida beaches" the rest of the time. The church will not gain worthy advances by shortcuts, magic formulas, or crash programs. It will not be nurtured through clever publicity, smart promotional schemes, or gimmicks. The laws of nature and the laws of the spiritual life will soon expose the careless and lazy sower.

THE EDUCATIONAL PROGRAM FOR STEWARDSHIP OF GIVING

If there is to be sufficient intake for generous stewardship output, a complete educational program will be required every year. The seed will be sown inadequately if educational contacts are cut short. They are necessary for a bountiful harvest.

The necessity of a comprehensive plan of education, such as the one that follows, may be questioned. The Holy Spirit, however, has put forth this principle in scripture: "Sow a little, reap a little—sow a lot, reap a lot." Those who have faithfully sown the seed of God's Word in an effective educational program have seen a drastic change and growth of understanding, attitude, and action of Christian stewards.

Successful congregations vary their programs and methods, but whatever approach they use, they organize it well to reach all members with a biblical message. They may use an "Every Member Contact" or group discussion meetings or another method, but always they plan well and execute their plan effectively so that all members are reached with the message. Recalling farmer Jim in his commitment to reach and care for every acre and every plant, church leaders will want to adopt some kind of "guidance system" which will reach every member, not overlooking anyone.

A four-week series of sermons and Bible studies on a special theme have proven valuable. Through experience and field-testing, it has been seen that concentrated periods of time are valuable for the process of building understanding and interest. Leaders schedule four Sundays for this conditioning phase, at which time sermons, Bible studies, lay talks, and children's object lessons are presented. This important preparation time conditions members to meditate on four vital aspects of a specific stewardship theme.

The *Stewardship Growth Series*, published by Neibauer Press,[1] complete with guidebooks, offers sermon outlines, Bible study outlines, lay talks, and children's object lessons. Four of the stewardship books and resources are primary sources for programs in the congregation: (1) *New Beginnings…in Christian Living and Giving*—Four weeks of messages and studies with a tithing emphases, including sample newsletter articles, letters and commitment cards. (2) *Big Step Forward in Faith*—Eight messages and studies that can be selectively used in the congregation's stewardship emphasis. (3) *Lord, Let It Happen to Me as You Said!*—Six messages and a booklet that outline God's plan for Christian service and giving. (4) *I Am Ready to Live*—Six messages and a booklet that challenge Christians to live purposely—not just exist—to give first fruits, not leftovers.

The same amount of energy used in maintenance programs for financial survival needs to be redirected toward the educational process. The same intensity once directed toward fund-raising efforts and special campaigns needs to be focused on basic biblical education.

Charlie Shedd's educational principle is a good approach for stewardship efforts in the church: "Study-the-scriptures-and-see-what-God-says-to-you…Start-somewhere-and-develop-as-the-Lord-leads." This is the goal of these series of four sermons and Bible studies for teaching the principles of Christian stewardship and giving.

The difference between traditional and scriptural giving can be seen in these two scenarios:

Scenario One—Leaders go to members to tell them about the financial needs of the church. The budget and ministries are explained in glowing terms. Members are urged to give generous gifts in a fund-raising program. They are approached as ones to supply the needs for the ministries of the church, and are told this will be possible only if they will consider larger contributions.

Scenario Two—Leaders go as God's priests to present a scriptural message. Members are told of how God calls them to ministry. They hear what God has done by His grace to make this possible. They are reached as people whose faith in Christ is to be expressed generously in the use of their abilities, possessions, and incomes. They are informed effectively about first fruits, generous, proportionate giving accomplished by the grace of God.

In the first scenario, people believe they are **donors** who are expected to meet the budget and needs of the church. In the second scenario, people see God speaking to them through their leaders. They see themselves as **disciples** and desire to be who God has made them to be.

The task is much greater than adding a few dollars to the church treasury each year. Stewardship of giving is not a matter of raising money only, but of raising people together with their money. Paul put it this way: "I don't want your possessions. Instead, I want you" (2 Corinthians 12:14). He was showing that the Christian giving approach is to the whole person through the Word. Paul was asking for much more than a financial response. For Paul, giving is a matter of "hearts for God" rather than "money for the church."

ADOPT A SEED-PLANTING, NURTURING SYSTEM

In the process of transforming a church from stewardship harvesting to seed-planting, it is especially urgent to pursue the biblical approach in Christian giving. Reaching all disciples, teaching them the biblical truths of Christian giving, provides fruit not possible with energy spent in donor fund-raising. There is a big difference between human approaches and biblical approaches in these matters.

	HARVESTING FOCUS	SEED-PLANTING FOCUS
1	Asks God to bless what the church is doing	Asks God to enable the church to do ministries He is blessing
2	Is overwhelmed by financial shortages and retreats from ministry opportunities	Adopts the seed-planting educational system in the face of financial shortages
3	Remains with the status quo of donor appeals	Plans new steps of faith by God's grace
4	Generates regular fund-raising projects to meet financial needs	Reaches all members through careful seed-planting and nurturing
5	Directs fund-raising programs through stewardship volunteers	Plants seeds and cultivates the soil through equipped leaders

Which is your approach? The material kingdom which is a failed legal system of expectations on the basis of try-a-little-harder, maintain the church and hope for the best or the kingdom where God is never short in supply of His provisions and always generous with His love? Breakthrough leaders will opt for reaching disciples by stewardship nurture, not "reaping" tactics. They understand this as an issue of doing it God's way, not the human way. They follow the Holy Spirit's guidance rather than human engineering. They have the courage to be obedient to the Word. They know, accept, and adopt the biblical system.

Along with the necessary biblical principles of Christian giving, people need to be taught financial planning and money management. Crown Financial Ministries[2] has developed a church manual and church training video that assists in implementing an important church small group study program. The highly productive book, *Small-Group Studies*, is designed to be led and administered by the local church. The aim of Crown Financial Ministries is to teach people God's financial principles through effective small group Bible study. Participants learn what scripture teaches about managing their possessions. The studies include topics discussing the earning of money, getting out of debt, spending, budgeting, saving, investing, giving, and training children.

The Crown study is very practical. Each time a principle is learned, it is applied. Those who have gone through the study have testified that their marriages have been strengthened and freed of debt. Graduates have become consistent savers, generous givers, and prudent consumers. Most importantly, people have entered into a closer relationship with Jesus Christ as they learn to apply the Word.

MAKE GRACE COMMITMENTS FOR INCREASING THE PERCENTAGE OF GIVING

Harvesters determine their offerings to God by the requirements of a budget or the church's demands to make a pledge. Such legalistic or law giving is characteristic of a traditional, maintenance, church. Seed-planting churches follow Paul's "grace system" of giving as God has given by the strength He gives. It is much easier to listen to stories of church ministry needs and pledges and fund-raising needed to support them than it is to make a commitment to give proportionately and generously. The biblical process, as described, is an educational process that requires the exercise of the mind and then the commitment of the heart.

Yakov Smirnoff, a Russian immigrant comic correctly enunciated, "The human spirit is not measured by the size of the act, but by the size of the heart." Converting this truth into biblical and church language, it can be affirmed, "The Christian call to stewardship is not measured by the size of the service or gift, but by the size of the heart." Far too often, financial pledges in fund-raising have been measured by the mind with a nudge from a loving heart. Stewardship of giving in the seed-planting church is first an exercise of the mind to determine the truth of God's teachings in the light of the financial resources God has given. This is followed by the commitment of the heart filled with and guided by God's explosive love for His people in Christ Jesus. Surely, the decision for the size of gifts is not to be made by the mind, but by the heart.

Exercise of the mind, mentioned before, is required to decide the portion to be given to God. The question must be asked: "What does God want?" Certainly God asks more of His people than to merely meet a church budget. Most budgets can be met when people give an average of 2 $^1/_2$ percent of their income to God—mere leftovers!

What is the practical and reasonable biblical thing to do in preparing people for making a financial commitment? Every member must first be educated in the biblical principles of giving. Four weeks of sermons and Bible studies can be planned, together with group meetings or contacts with all members, to review the biblical principles in giving. Resources like *New Beginnings and Big Step Forward in Faith*[3] can be used. Whether for group meetings or individual contacts, stewardship messages like those found in booklets like *Big Step Forward in Faith, I Am Ready to Live, or Lord, Let It Happen to Me as You Said*[4] are valuable. Whatever plan is used, it is important to make certain that the message contains the giving principles outlined in God's Word. That plan includes these five principles:

(1) Give to God **first**, before buying groceries, clothes, car, and making mortgage payments. Jesus said, "But first, be concerned about His kingdom and what has His approval. Then all these things will be provided for you" (Matthew 6:33).

(2) Give a planned percentage or portion of all income to Christ's church. 1 Corinthians 16:2 says, "Every Sunday each of you should set aside some of your money and save it. Then money won't have to be collected when I come." Both Old and New Testaments emphasize a portion or part to be set aside for God's work—the sacred part, separated for kingdom tasks.

(3) Give a generous percentage to God. New Testament believers will prayerfully consider whether they will give more or less than God's people in the Old Testament—ten cents out of each dollar. To give a small portion is contrary to the new nature in Christ. To give a generous part, ten percent and more, is a true expression of the "Christ in us." Tithing in itself is an inadequate expression of faith. God requires more of His people than ten percent of their income. Also, tithing is not a legalistic rule, for grace disallows any standard to condemn or threaten. The tithe is to guide and encourage.

(4) Give a set percentage amount for Christ's kingdom **by faith**. God says, "Managers are required to be trustworthy" (1 Corinthians 4:2)—full of faith. The weaker the faith, the lower the percentage. The stronger the faith, the higher the percentage. While God does not give a law (under grace) as to what exact percentage will please Him, growing faith will be expressed in a growing percentage.

Some are giving three cents or less of every dollar of income. Others are giving five or seven cents, and some ten and fifteen cents of every dollar. Whatever portion or percentage, believers will ask themselves whether this part is the true measure of their faith and love. As each

Christian grows in faith, he or she will give a larger portion. The prayer must be, "Lord, increase my faith."

(5) Give a generous percentage as a **grace** from God. Paul said, "Brothers and sisters, we want you to know how God showed his kindness to the churches in the province of Macedonia. While they were being severely tested by suffering, their overflowing joy, along with their extreme poverty, has made them even more generous" (2 Corinthians 8:1-2). Generous proportionate giving is a gift (grace) from God for which each Christian should pray. Christ's love compels believers to give that way. The question is: What is the proper response by God's grace?

ALL MEMBERS ARE TO MAKE A STEWARDSHIP COMMITMENT

It is vital that every Christian make a definite commitment. A percentage of one's income for God is to be used for God. The old nature always seeks to destroy any and all good intentions. But when a Christian predetermines what he or she will give God, the new nature "ties down" the old nature, so to speak. It settles the question before the old nature can try to go back to its old default.

The first part of the stewardship commitment is an exercise of the mind. Church members are to analyze their giving habits, understand them, and recognize what portion or percentage of their income they are giving to God. They are to consider increasing that percentage as their "above" offering for the ministries of the church. Meditating on the message that follows benefits this exercise of the mind.

Each person must concentrate on what it means to give a proportion of one's income as well as how it is to be measured. Since Christ's love compels Christians to grow in giving, they will want to increase the percentage they give to God. If persons are giving less than 10 percent to the Lord at this time, will they ask God for the grace and faith to increase it by 1, 2, 3, or 4 percent? If a person is giving 3 percent, will he or she be willing to increase it by 3 percent so that the first fruits are 6 percent in the future? Church members must pray for the strength to increase their giving by at least 1% of their personal income. If that seems difficult, they need to wrestle with God in prayer and ask the Holy Spirit for strength and the gift or grace of giving. If some persons give 10% or more, they may choose to ask God for the gift of increasing their giving by 1% of income. All persons in the seed-planting church are challenged to set aside at least 1% for the important world mission cause.

Individual persons or family units must take a close look at their personal finances and what they are giving God. Will they make a step of growth by going through this valuable exercise? These are the types of questions to be asked in the process:

Sample Gift Worksheet
a. My estimated annual income is: $ _____
b. A tithe (10%) of this would be: $ _____
c. My present weekly offerings are: $ _____
d. This amounts to an annual percentage of: $ _____
e. I will increase my giving by this percentage of my personal income (circle one).   1%   2%   3%   4% This will be a new % of _____ %
f. Based on this percentage total, my offering for next year will be: $ _____
g. This represents a weekly offering of about: $ _____
May God give you a strong faith to adopt priorities pleasing to Him!

This exercise of the mind is followed by a commitment of the heart. The Christian life, with its walk of faith, is not measured by the size of the stewardship action or gift, but by the size of the heart. A heart filled with Christ's love and expressed by Christian faith should guide each believer's commitment. A sample commitment follows:

Sample Personal Commitment Form

I thank God, who has blessed me with all spiritual blessings in Jesus Christ (Ephesians 1:3). By His grace and the Holy Spirit's strength, and because of Jesus' love for me, I seek to put God first as the priority in my life. I plan to take new steps of faith in these areas:

1. I desire to grow and mature spiritually

   _____ To renew my spiritual energy through personal and group Bible study

   _____ To worship and commune regularly at the Lord's table

2. I desire to be a functioning member of Christ's body

   _____ To use my spiritual gifts and abilities in ministries of the church as opportunities are available

   _____ To share the gospel and witness of my Christian faith

3. I desire to manage my financial resources well and to give faithfully to God. I will make the following commitment (mark with an X or numerical response):

   (1) ___ I will give 10% (a tithe) of my income.

   (2) ___ I am giving less than 10% and will increase my gift to _____% of my income.

   (3) ___ I give 10% or more and will increase my percentage by _____%.

   (4) ___ I will begin first fruit proportionate giving, sharing a percentage of my total personal income. This represents my growing faith, will glorify Christ, and works to advance His kingdom.

Signed: _____

FOLLOW BASIC STEWARDSHIP PRINCIPLES

Universal principles help members of the body grow in stewardship quality and quantity. Stewardship leaders will want to master these key stewardship principles and apply them in the work of the church:

(1) The Scripture Principle—God's Word is the only guide for stewardship decisions and is the food to nurture faith for generous giving.

(2) The Basic Principle—God has given His people all the spiritual and material resources required to bring the saving gospel of Jesus Christ to all people in the world in our lifetime.

(3) The Growth Principle—Evaluating the process, setting goals, and adopting effective strategies enables the church to make maximum use of God's Word for maximum results for stewardship growth of God's people.

(4) The Priority Principle—God's people are to "seek God first" in everything and realize that the first, big stewardship offering is the repentant heart.

(5) The People Principle—Effective stewardship efforts are people-centered, not program-centered. Only as persons are led to identify their spiritual gifts and abilities for ministries can the church minister aggressively.

(6) The Supply Principle—"God's work done in God's way will never lack God's supply" (J. Hudson Taylor).

(7) The Simplicity Principle—The best method is as little method as possible.

(8) The Timing principle—Successful work is done only when believers work in harmony with God's time table and seek His guidance through prayer.

These principles help believers grow in the grace of stewardship. Planting and nurturing stewardship seeds results in abundant harvests. Leaders will want to master these key stewardship principles and apply them in the stewardship training of the Church. Stewardship education to strengthen our spiritual life and fruitfulness! It will result in worshipful living that compels Christians to bring their lives and gifts to the altar! It will grow abundant numbers of believers demonstrating true discipleship! In the end, it will produce God's kind of harvest!

CHAPTER 6

The Seed-Planting, Nurturing Church Cares for the Entire Field

Farmer Jim concentrates his time and efforts on raising healthy plants in his field. In the same way, pastors and church leaders are called to build healthy members and relationships in the church. The church is God's field. Growing healthy relationships enables all persons to be cared for in God's field.

An unhealthy pastor or leader hurts the congregation by manipulating, over-controlling, or by neglecting those over which he has been placed. On the other hand, healthy pastors and healthy leaders grow healthy people. Healthy pastors minister grace and healing to the people. They give them much needed nourishment and direction. They nurture healthy relationships that grow healthy members.

The Trinity is relational. God the Father, the Son, and the Holy Spirit are in a functional, integral relationship for eternity. The relationships found in the Church are to be a model and extension of the Trinity. They are possible only because of the health that exists in the Trinity itself. The Triune God builds His relationships with His people through the sacraments and the Word. By His grace He forgives their sins, restores their relationship with Him, and communicates with them by His love—in His Church, the community of faith.

Relationships are the foundation of pastoral and lay ministry. Christian relationships impact the ministries of the church at every point. What believers do flows out of their being rightly connected to one another in Christ. This requires biblical integrity in all relationships. It must be recognized that the body of Christ precedes and actually directs the church organization and its programs. When bureaucracy rules or structures get out of control, the community of faith suffers. It becomes institutionalized. Church organization must never overpower the organism, the body of Christ.

Since Paul's day, the historic struggle of the church (related to function and form) has been the tension between the body of Christ and its institutional form. Jesus made one simple announcement: "I will build My Church" (Matthew 16:18). It is not my church or yours. The Church, after all, is not a human organization, but one divinely planned and called into being.

God called the Church together in Christ to be "…a spiritual house that is being built into a holy priesthood…" (1 Peter 2:5). It is the community of Christ's believers on earth. "God has put everything under the control of Christ. He has made Christ the Head of everything for the good of the Church" (Ephesians 1:22).

Believers are together identified as the family of God. "I will be your Father, and you will be My sons and daughters" (2 Corinthians 6:18). Their highest title is not as church members, but as God's children. "He gave the right to become God's children to everyone who believed in Him" (John 1:12).

Each member of the Church—the body of Christ—is valuable and interdependent. Each member is united by the Spirit and thereby committed to truth. He or she is equipped to serve, motivated and filled by Christ's love. Each member of the body functions according to his or her sanctified design. To be true to the Head, no person can live as though he or she is the whole body. Believers cannot be uninvolved in the needs and suffering of those in the Church or in the world.

Christ is the unifier and coordinator as the body carries out its functions. The head gives life to His Church, guiding and controlling it. Mutual responsibility and interdependence of individual members of the body is best seen in the "one another" passages of the epistles:

- "Love each other as I have loved you" (John 15:12).
- "…Even though we are many individuals, Christ makes us one body and individuals who are connected to each other" (Romans 12:5).
- "Be devoted to each other like a loving family" (Romans 12:10).
- "Accept each other in the same way that Christ accepted you" (Romans 15:7).
- "I'm also convinced…that you are able to instruct each other" (Romans 15:14).
- "Serve each other through love" (Galatians 5:13).

- "Help carry each other's burdens" (Galatians 6:2).
- "Be patient with each other and lovingly accept each other" (Ephesians 4:2).
- "Encourage each other and strengthen each other as you are doing" (1 Thessalonians 5:11).
- "Admit your sins to each other, and pray for each other…" (James 5:16).

No person is complete by oneself and no one has been entrusted with all. Completeness is found only in mutual sharing and caring through the Christian community. The Church exists only in community.

It is also true, though, that no Christian community can be fully healthy and have no spiritually sick members. If the Christian community is to be a safe place for even the weakest, it must be a place where persons are safe to express pain and hurt. The church must be a place where people can get help and support for heartache and abuse. No one should be left in despair. No one should be left to believe that they themselves are the problem because they do not have enough faith. No wrongs or pains should be ignored. The healthy community of faith addresses hurts and wrongs in people's lives rather than "wallpapering" over them or hiding them under a rug.

Good communication is necessary for a healthy community of faith. This is true between the pastor and his people as well as from person to person. Each member must have access to each other without restrictions. Good communication demands that there are no locks on doors of contact. No door dare be slammed in any face. There will always be an open door to each other.

Spiritual transformation happens most compellingly and completely in the context of Christian community. A healthy community will see people connected and transparent. It will deal with unhealthy relationships. Above all, through the sharing of God's Word with each other, Christ will be incarnated into the community.

CARING FOR ALL MEMBERS OF THE CHURCH

Pastors and leaders must be conscious that God has given them, just as He had given Paul, the care of the churches. "…I have the daily pressure of my anxiety about all the churches" (2 Corinthians 11:28). For three full years Paul had instructed the Ephesians "day and night, at times with tears in my eyes" (Acts 20:31). The responsibility to lead the church faithfully is serious business! Paul told the believers at Philippi that they should be "...firmly united in spirit, united in fighting for the faith that the good news brings" (Philippians 1:27).

Paul was concerned. He wanted each member to receive spiritual insight and understanding and see things from God's point of view. He wanted each member to make his or her life purposeful, to be active and fruitful in ministry. As Paul said, every Christian lives, moves, and exists because of Christ (Acts 17:28). When Christ is within, a new person exists! The Spirit then prompts Christians to care for one another as Christ cares for them. Disconnected believers, in and of themselves, evidence the fact that they have not taken the gospel seriously. Paul told believers to nurture each other, by God's grace, in Christ's love. Paul's ministry was all about connecting the people of the Church through their faith.

MEMBER'S MINISTRY TO EACH OTHER BY A SMALL GROUP OR CELL CHURCH PLAN-STRATEGY

Jethro's principle of ministry to the people involved the appointing of leaders over 10, 50, 100 and 1000. Jesus' ministry began by selecting a group of 12, whom He sent out to spread the good news (Mark 3:14). He continued meeting with small groups many times. Pentecost happened in a house where the disciples were meeting (Acts 2:2). The apostles taught house to house (Acts 5:42). Paul and Silas went to Lydia's house (Acts 20:20). Paul asked the Roman Christians to greet the people that met in the house of Priscilla and Aquila (Romans 16:5). Paul sent greetings to the brothers and sisters in Laodicia that met in Nympha's house (Colossians 4:15) and to the believers who met in Philemon's house (Philemon 1).

Ephesians 4:12-16 shows that each member is to build up and care for each other. Every current and new member should be recruited into the spiritual force in homes for equipping the saints. The small groups that met in the house in Antioch (Acts 11) built a new church but also spread the good news in many other places. Small groups and cell churches, where God's Word is central, facilitate ministry mobilization of each believer. This creates an environment for believers to function effectively and minister more aggressively. It allows quicker expansion of the leadership base by developing leaders in an equipping mode.

Meeting in small groups encourages changes to take place in which God's Word challenges people's spirituality and value systems. It allows discipleship to happen in the context of body-life. It helps advance the use of gifts and grace given to us "for the common good" (1 Corinthians 12:7). It is a "relationship oriented" approach which builds a seed-planting, nurturing, missional church. It also provides an environment where non-believing friends can experience the presence and power of God in Christ Jesus.

LESSONS FROM THE BERRY PATCH

Paul would no doubt be comfortable with the lessons learned from the person who tends a raspberry patch. The mind is quick to imagine a harvester standing at the edge of the berry field with his bushels of ripe fruit. But as any farmer knows, harvesting berries depends upon healthy plants—and considerable preparation. Every spring he tears out dead raspberry canes and trims back the new ones. Having done his part, the sun and rain must "do their thing." Fertilizer provides food and enriches the plants. Warmer weather brings new leaves and blossoms.

God's creation works miraculously to bring about an annual harvest. Once the berries are ripe, it's time to plunge into the prickly patch and gather them. Some are not easily seen. Because they ripen under the leaves, the picker must search, moving branches as he or she goes along. At times, hard work uncovers the most sumptuous berries! But if the farmer doesn't look for the fruit regularly, he will lose some of the harvest. He will lose some of it to natural forces of decay. And of course, the birds get their fair share. The berries, because they do not mature at the same time, produce a new crop each day.

Preparation and outreach are needed for the harvest of souls. The berry patch offers both lessons and principles. (1) Not one thing can happen apart from God. (2) If a harvest is to be expected, dead canes will have to be removed. Dead traditions, methodologies, and strategies must be seriously pruned in order to produce a healthy church. (3) Healthy plants must be carefully imbedded in nutritious soil. Members must be carefully infused in a healthy community. (3) The entire patch or field must be tended in order to produce best results. All plants must be carefully fertilized, trimmed, and nurtured. (4) Timing is critical. The work must be done when pruning is required and also when the "fruit" is ready. (5) Pickers must go out into "the patch" if they want to harvest "berries." They cannot be content to remain in comfort. (6) They must be persistent in order to witness the greatest harvest.

Whether vegetable, grain, fruit, or members of a church, the principles remain the same.[1] The best way to get the "berry patch" ready and to enjoy the harvest is to have others join the work force. Every Christian is a laborer. Some are better prepared than others, but this is not the task of a pastor or church leaders alone. Christ's people must be ready to get their hands dirty, facing the prickles and bugs of the patch.

There is one big lesson for the church and its leaders. Members need to be out of their pews! God wanted the disciples out of the comfort of Jerusalem—so that the gospel would spread! In the same way, He wants church members out of the cathedral-barn into the fields—so ministry can spread! For the disciples, the human tendency was to "hang out" in Jerusalem, just soaking up the blessings. But in Acts 7 and 8, everything changed quickly. "Widespread persecution broke out against the church in Jerusalem. Most believers, except the apostles, were scattered throughout Judea and Samaria" (Acts 8:1). It was persecution that got them "out of their pews!"

The "party," the time of rest, is over for the Church today. It does not need, however, to wait for a time of persecution in order to begin. From scripture, the imperatives of seedtime and harvest are clear. Church leadership is not merely about receiving from heaven, but about sharing heaven's life with the people of the church in the world. The work force described in Acts 8:4 was mobile! "The believers who were scattered went from place to place, where they spread the Word." Churches and members are called to go beyond the comfortable zone of liturgies, pews, programs, and institutional securities.

RETAINING THE FAITHFUL—RECLAIMING THE INACTIVE

In Ephesians 4:15-16, Paul describes a church life in which members lovingly speak the truth of God's Word to one another. This begins a continual process that allows members to grow up in their relationship to Christ, who is the head. It allows the whole body to fit together, united through the support of each of these members. As each part of the organism does its job, the body grows and builds itself up in love. This process begins with the pastor, continues on to family members in homes, and expands to the entire church, each being priests to each other.

The intensity of the response to God's Word and the life of fellowship varies in congregations. Some have a low level of faith and commitment. They neglect the means whereby God's grace is bestowed on them. Church leaders must mediate Christ's love to members, feeding all, strengthening the weak. In that way, they minister by the Holy Spirit, nourishing and reinforcing persons in faith through effective ministry of the Word. While published communications are vital, the Word is best embodied in spiritual leaders who reach individual members at the point of need.

SPECIAL FEEDING AND CARE FOR THE WEAK

Churches that tend to wholesale their communications—using mainly written letters, or e-mail, neglecting individual contacts—fail in their scriptural responsibilities. The care with which the sender conveys the message is a factor that critically affects how well the Word will be received. From a biblical standpoint, the failure to foster love, to give careful attention to the weak and troubled, is a scandal to the gospel. Pastors and spiritual leaders far too often become defeated in their attempts to reach marginal members effectively. In fact, traditional attempts are to send a letter or an elder with a reminder that they need to attend church. After awhile, these persons are simply dropped from the church roster. Does this not grieve the Good Shepherd of the flock?

The seed-planting, nurturing church will acknowledge the situation, face the facts, and begin with building healthy leaders. It will begin with those who are spiritually strong and able to tend the field properly. What will such spiritual leaders offer "helpless" members and their anemic spirituality? They must learn to adopt the biblical pattern of tending and caring for fragile plants in God's field. The spiritually powerless need the loving support and encouragement of strong spiritual leaders.

THE NEED FOR RESTRAINT OR CORRECTION

Jesus gave instructions on how to deal with situations that require correction and restraint (sometimes called "church discipline"). He told His disciples how to deal with erring or straying members (Matthew 18:15-18). The purpose of such spiritual correction and redirection is positive. It should express the grace of God and restore the errant member. Every Christian congregation should practice such loving guidance. Why?

1. *To restore* a person who is doing wrong (Galatians 6:1, Matthew 6:14-15).

2. *To correct* an offense and remove temptation (1 Corinthians 8:9).

3. *To maintain* the Christian testimony of the church (1 Timothy 3:7).

4. *To encourage* every member to remain faithful (1 Corinthians 5:6-7).

Such spiritual correction should not be considered punishment. The church is not the agent to punish a guilty person for not seeking the forgiveness of Christ. In Matthew 18, Jesus gave specific guidelines for dealing with a believer who has erred. The steps are simple. Any difficulty should be corrected privately by a member who is aware of the problem, or between persons who are involved. If this personal encounter does not solve the problem, two or three others should be asked to help get to the root of the matter. If the offending person still refuses to repent, the matter is to be taken to the spiritual leaders of the church. The aim is to arouse the conscience of the unrepentant one. He or she needs to be reminded of how serious this action is to their relationship with Christ.

If persons are excluded from the congregation, scripture says they should not be treated as troublemakers, but should be sought in love. The purpose is to win them back through repentance and forgiveness in Christ (2 Thessalonians 3:15, James 5:19-20). Then these persons should be taken into full fellowship and again be assured of full forgiveness (2 Corinthians 2:6-7, Galatians 6:1-2). All of this must be done in the spirit of meekness and love in order to restore them to full relationship with Christ and the church.

Any church that compromises at this point denies the perfect character of God and does not fulfill His purpose for the fellowship of the church. That church then loses its testimony to the world. The church community is required to establish certain standards as a response to God's Word. Compromise opens the door to divisions and separations, and to offense in the church and outside. The fellowship of the church must center on a living relationship with God and each other, the kind of relationship God intended.

The Lord does not hold a church responsible for results, but rather for its obedience in patient and persistent contact with weak members. The inactive member, basically unattended in many churches, is one of the most important objects of ministry of the church. As the treasurer's books are meticulously audited, accounting for every penny, the congregation needs to be equally concerned about accounting for each soul that God has committed to its care.

Twenty-five percent or more of the members of maintenance, harvesting congregations can be classified as inactive or spiritually weak. They habitually neglect God's Word and worship, estranging themselves from Christian fellowship. Tragically, hundreds of thousands of people are simply dropped from church membership each year. This situation is aggravated by the fact that church rolls continue to carry the names of many more members who give little evidence of spirituality. Weak, lethargic members of the body of Christ are slow to believe and are not feeding on the Word. The greatest disservice done to inactive Christians is to let them drift away from Christ, unaware of how they are harming themselves. How is it possible for church leaders to sit idly by and watch people afloat spiritually because of a disregard of the Savior?

Are church leaders prepared to hear a shocking truth? Farmer Jim would obviously be out of business if he failed to tend to 25 percent of his total crop. Is the situation so hopeless in the church that it cannot care for the weak and dying, those in "the revolving door?" Are all in God's field safe?

SOME SPIRITUAL IMPERATIVES

God's Word contains many examples of His passion to reach those who have drifted out of fellowship with Him. Luke 15 reveals Christ's intense concern for weak and wandering Christians in three parables. The story of the lost sheep typifies a believer lost in the wilderness of sin, separated from the Good Shepherd and His flock. That one must be found and brought back. God counts each individual. He is concerned about a one percent loss and greatly celebrates when one returns.

Jesus' story about the lost coin characterizes those who are still in the church but are not seen. They have not left the church, but have been "out of sight." It will take some looking and sweeping, but they can be found and restored to a vital relationship to Christ and His kingdom. Again, God rejoices when members change the way they think and act in His kingdom.

The parable of the lost son exemplifies those who have willfully left their father's house and are harming themselves by their lifestyle. Church leaders need to seek and reach these with a loving touch and forgiveness in Christ. The wandering ones need to hear welcoming words that invite repentance and celebrate the prospect of renewed fellowship. An anxious Father openly and eagerly awaits their return—so must the church.

Jesus showed concern for fruitless Christians by using the illustration of a fruitless fig tree. The owner said to the gardener, "For the last three years I've come to look for figs on this fig tree but haven't found any. Cut it down! Why should it use up good soil?" The gardener replied, "Sir, let it stand for one more year. I'll dig around it and fertilize it. Maybe next year it'll have figs. But if not, then cut it down" (Luke 13:6-9).

The gardener's answer gives a clue to church leaders' responsibility toward inactive and weak members in the congregation's orchard. The gardener pleaded that the tree be spared one more year while he gave it special attention, digging around it and feeding it. The spiritual imperative is clear: cultivate each inactive member carefully. That is God's call to gardeners in His fields.

SYMPTOMS AND CAUSES OF WEAK SPIRITUALITY

Church leaders need to recognize the common symptoms of persons who are spiritually weak, sick, or drifting away from Christ:

1. They do not worship or commune regularly. They neglect God's Word and habitually disregard Christian practices (Luke 11:28, Acts 2:42, Hebrews 10:25).

2. They do not lead a godly life and do not conform to the will of Christ (John 15:6-8, Galatians 5:19-26, James 1:22).

3. They do not believe or accept the basic beliefs and doctrines of scripture (John 8:31, 47; 2 John 9).

4. They are wrapped up in self and materialism, having little interest in the spiritual life (Matthew 16:26, 22:37-38, 1 Timothy 6:10, 1 John 2:15).

5. They do not accept the ministry of the pastor and spiritual leaders, no longer desiring fellowship in the church (Hebrews 10: 24-25, James 5:16).

The basic reasons for spiritual problems in the lives of Christians are the attacks of the devil, the world, and the sinful self. They present strong temptations, induce uncertainty of faith, and lead a person into sinful habits. Worldly attitudes may be a factor, as well as a number of other possible reasons.

Psychological reasons—The ideals of the church may seem too difficult for some persons to meet. The pressures and pace of their days may crowd God out of their life. On the other hand, members may feel that they do not fit in the church and have a sense of inadequacy. Some may feel not wanted, or have feelings of inferiority or insecurity.

Theological reasons—Many persons lack adequate knowledge and understanding of God's Word. The church may have failed to challenge these persons to truly believe God, to understand that they can truly live by faith. They may have grown very little spiritually since they became church members. Some have never fully understood the gospel itself. They may have received a superficial type of instruction as a new member. Or there may have been good instruction but they never had a clear understanding of God's will or His will for their lives. A sense of guilt may keep them from realizing a close fellowship with God. Doctrinal difficulties and doubts may have been ignored or answered superficially, later raising serious questions about the Christian faith. Others may not have an understanding of grace and Christian freedom, and become legalistic.

Cultural or sociological reasons—Weak or inactive members may have a sense of not being wanted or needed. Other church members may have failed to help them appreciate true fellowship in the church. Some may feel that the church fences them in, restricting their freedom and action. The careless morals and low standards of modern society may have made them callous to God's law so that they cannot see themselves as God sees them.

Economic reasons—Christian stewardship and giving, if not properly presented or understood, can become a source of personal objection or sense of guilt. Many have not received the proper scriptural teaching and motivation for Christian stewardship and giving and may have been perceived as being too need-centered or budget-centered. As a result, resentment grows against the church about seemingly unreasonable financial demands.

Personal reasons—There may be actual or fancied personal misunderstandings between members, a pastor, a relative, or an organization in the church. Families may be experiencing breakdowns in relations. Some may have allowed the worries of life or worldly desires to destroy the good seed of the Word so that they bear little or no fruit. There may be a fear of losing out on some of life's pleasures. Some have been conquered by a sinful habit that is inconsistent with their Christian discipleship. Instead of rejecting the habit, they give up their faith and church. Others have wrong expectations and become dissatisfied with the church and its people.

THE RECLAIMING AND REBUILDING PROCESS

Imagine if one-fourth of a person's home was unstable and in danger of collapse. Would he ignore the problem? If one-fourth of the employees in a person's business were unreliable, having erratic attendance and performance, would he remain silent? If one of a father's four children came home only to sleep and eat, exhibiting an ungodly lifestyle, would he dispassionately allow it? Certainly, it would not be normal for any of these persons to throw up his hands and say it was out of his control, that there was nothing he could do. The normal person would act!

As the church looks at those for whom God has made it responsible, what kind of reclaiming or rebuilding plan will it adopt? As a person would renovate his home, as he would retrain his employees, as he would vision a new lifestyle with his child, so the church must be ready to take ownership of weak and inactive members.

The responsibility for winning back weak and inactive members belongs to the whole church. The pastor, as spiritual leader, is to guide and love according to the truths expressed in Matthew 18. The pastor's first responsibility should be to build up a spirit of genuine Christian concern among all members of the congregation. The elders, deacons, or spiritual leaders should be especially active in personal contacts.

The pastor and spiritual leaders may conduct a series of special fellowship gatherings which present specific messages on how to build and maintain a personal relationship with Christ. The entire congregation may be invited or smaller groups of about ten family units at a time. Not all will respond to such an invitation, but they must be made nonetheless. Some may respond to small group interactive Bible studies involving about ten people, including both spiritually strong, active members and weaker, inactive members. No matter which approach is used, God's people need to be united in finding His will concerning every member in the church.

Most important is the matter of enlisting shepherds for weak or inactive members. In most congregations, there will be so many to be reached that it is not practical or possible to shepherd them all effectively, even within one or two years. But the process must be begun. The church must first enlist and equip spiritually strong leaders and members for the task of shepherding. A series of meetings could be used for this process, including an interactive Bible study like the *Spiritual Travel Guide*[2]. When the shepherd has sufficient experience with one person, he or she could add a second and even third person for whom to be responsible. More and more spiritual leaders and members must be enlisted and equipped to be shepherds of individual and small groups of weak and inactive members so that within two or three years all are cared for.

The first step is to count! The membership rolls must be studied carefully and prayerfully in order to identify weak and inactive members who need tending. They must be listed by name. The church must take responsibility and be held accountable for them. God has placed them under the care of individual laborers that He has called to His field.

The process begins by caring for these one by one, two by two, then by tens, by twenties. Every time one person becomes active in Bible study, worship, and fellowship, leaders can celebrate! No matter whether the gatherings are of the pastoral staff, spiritual leaders, or shepherds, the group can celebrate! In the movie *A Wonderful Life*, a bell rings every time an angel gets his wings. What about ringing a bell in the spiritual leaders' meetings every time a member is won back to spiritual strength and is again active in the body of Christ? The action would be an audible reminder of the Luke 15 rejoicing when any person comes back, changing the way he thinks and acts! Yes, all heaven rejoices (Luke 15: 7, 10)!

A schedule can be worked out for regularly calling each inactive member. Monthly meetings can give reports on calls that have been made and plan the kind of visits to be made in the future. Careful records must be kept. The process must continue until all members are safe in a shepherding plan.

THE MESSAGE FOR THE RECLAIMING AND REBUILDING PROCESS

Shepherds should not beg people to come to church or give them the impression that that's what church membership is about. Instead, shepherds should help them realize the rich benefits of maintaining a close relationship with Christ.

Heart-sharing is vital. If persons have a grievance, shepherds must listen patiently, restate the problem, urge them to share their concerns, and pray. Shepherds need to provide a simple, clear grace message that embodies the basis of both salvation and living the Christian life. They must stress the need for understanding, grace, repentance, and forgiveness (Colossians 3:3-13). The discussion must be kept positive and on a spiritual level at all times. Shepherds must deal with excuses cautiously, looking for the real reason behind the excuse. They must ask the Holy Spirit to work through them, providing them with light from the scriptures in answering questions and dealing with problems.

Shepherds can offer to leave devotional guides with the person or family. They can tell the person about Bible study opportunities at the church, especially ones that are interactive. Some may be invited to participate in Christian service opportunities.

Shepherds help the person to understand that Christianity and church membership are not the same. Membership is not just a matter of attending church, but of maintaining a strong relationship with God in Jesus Christ. The conversation should center on the major issues of the Christian faith. If the person sounds as if he or she is depending too much on external factors—good actions in life, having good Christian parents, etc.—the shepherd can share an uplifting message of dependence on Christ for the grace that comes by Him alone.

It would be helpful to prepare a series of leading questions for the visit. As the person tries to answer such questions, he or she may realize certain failures in his or her thinking. The questions should lead the person to think about solutions. The shepherd's goal is not to get surface assent to religious propositions, but to help the person make a right decision and translate it into action. A message something like the following may be helpful:

"God has given each Christian a purpose and a mission in life. It may seem that you took the initiative to be a believer, but you were actually drawn to faith by a love far greater than any human force. When by God's grace you came to faith, you only may have been thinking of joining a church, but in reality you were becoming a part of the body of Christ. You were entering into a living relationship with Him. In 1 Corinthians 3, the Bible tells us that we are God's building, a temple of God. We belong to Christ (verses 3:9, 16, 23). Knowing this, what purpose do you believe God has for you? How is He to be the Lord of your life? How can you seek to grow in God's grace and be in closer relationship with God?" The shepherd can build a conversation around these biblical statements and questions.

If there are children in the family who should be attending Sunday school or youth gatherings, the shepherd should emphasize parental responsibilities. God has given parents the privileged opportunity and the divine responsibility for the spiritual training of their children. By involving children in Sunday school and other spiritual activities, parents will be building a healthy Christian climate in the home.

The shepherd needs to focus persons on the drawing power of Christ's love, the love that puts God at the center of their lives. He must emphasize the positive features of a truly Christian life. He must ask questions that probe and cause the person to think about certain priorities: "What do you as a family want most out of life? What place do you want to give Christ in your life? How can you show love and care in your home?"

THE MESSAGE FOR RECLAIMING INACTIVES: "COME HOME!"

During visits to inactive members, spiritual leaders can warmly invite them to "Come home!" This is an invitation to come home to God, to God's family, to peace and strength, to hope, to joy!

A good way to begin the conversation would be to talk about those who provide primary services—doctors, pharmacies, banks, policemen, firemen, government officials. Then go on to share the fact that no service provider can offer what the church provides.

Another "icebreaker" could revolve around the pictures of Thomas Kinkade or Norman Rockwell. Home should be a place for basic security, encouragement, affirmation, companionship, and kindness. But no home is perfect—or permanent. Some, unfortunately, are even harmful and offer little or no peace.

The church is the spiritual home that God provides all believers. It should also provide necessary security, encouragement, and love. In reality the church, like the family, is not perfect. It is made of sinners invited by God's grace, to become His children—each a sinner and a saint forgiven in Christ. Each is invited to "come home."

The invitation is not just to come home for Christmas, for Easter, for a marriage, or a baptism. It is an invitation to a spiritual "homecoming" that originates from God Himself. God welcomes every person—so does the church. God rejects no one—neither does the church. The peace, strength, hope, and joy in Christ that God offers is not received from a distance or by looking into a church window, but by being in contact with God's family. It is received by worshiping with fellow sinner-saints and by gathering with them in small Bible study groups. Coming home answers the most important question—the reason for and the purpose of life itself.

Come home to God, to His love and forgiveness. By coming home, what can be found? Unconditional love that will never end. A spiritual bond that cannot be severed. A relationship with Jesus that never can be broken. "…nothing can ever separate us from God's love which Christ Jesus our Lord shows us. We can't be separated by death or life, by angels or rulers, by anything in the present or anything in the future, by forces or powers in the world above or in the world below, or by anything else in creation" (Romans 8:38-39). In the church home, God tells members that they "are holy partners in a heavenly calling. So look carefully at Jesus...Encourage each other every day while you have the opportunity...we will remain Christ's partners only if we continue to hold on to our original confidence until the end" (Hebrews 3:1, 13-14).

There is no end to the love God shows those who come home to Him. "God has shown us His love by sending His only Son into the world so that we could have life through Him. This is love: not that we have loved God, but that He loved us and sent His Son to be the payment for our sins" (1 John 4:9-10). Parents, doctors, and government officials may sometimes fail. Church leaders may likewise disappoint. But God's Word promises that "all things work together for the good of those who love God—those whom He has called according to His plan" (Romans 8:28). *Come home to God!*

Come home to God's family! God's family (where He is Father and believers are His sons and daughters) is the spiritual home on earth where Christians offer each other the grace, mercy, and love that they have received from God. God has designed His family in such a way that members perform acts of love that meet each other's needs. "We understand what love is when we realize that Christ gave His life for us. This means we must give our life for other believers...we must love each other because love comes from God...if this is the way God loves us, we must also love each other" (1 John 3:16, 4:7, 11).

As believers come home to God's family, they look beyond personalities, failures, and weaknesses of other church members. "...though we are many individuals, Christ makes us one body and individuals who are connected to each other" (Romans 12:5). Because each believer is part of God's family, members are to "be devoted to each other like a loving family" (Romans 12:10). They are to "accept each other in the same way that Christ accepted you" (Romans 15:7). With their imperfections, they are to "be patient with each other and lovingly accept each other" (Ephesians 4:2).

No persons are complete by themselves. Completeness in God's family is found only in mutual sharing and caring through the community of faith. The community of faith is a safe place to express pain and hurt. The fact is, no individual is. So God's family is where people can get help and support for their heartaches, difficulties, and even abuse. God wants no one left in despair, but for all to come home to His family.

Come home to peace and strength! Coming home to God will give a peace that cannot be taken away. "Now that we have God's approval because of faith, we have peace with God because of what our Lord Jesus Christ has done. Through Christ we can approach God and stand in His favor" (Romans 5:1-2). Jesus, our loving Savior, invites us: "Come to me, all who are tired from carrying heavy loads, and I will give you rest. Place my yoke over your shoulders, and learn from me, because I am gentle and humble. Then you will find rest for yourselves" (Matthew 11:28-29). This type of message is transmitted through the voices of Christians, but it is the Word, the promise of God itself, that "gives strength to those who grow tired and increases the strength of those who are weak" (Isaiah 40:29). Whatever circumstances the inactives may encounter, the leader should assure them that the brothers and sisters in God's family "ask God to strengthen you by His glorious might with all the power you need to patiently endure everything with joy" (Galatians 1:11).

Come home to hope and joy! The leader may conclude by sharing that the members of God's family are praying, "May God, the source of hope, fill you with joy and peace through your faith in Him. Then you will overflow with hope by the power of the Holy Spirit" (Romans 15:13). Leaders may share, "There is realistic hope for your future!" If the inactives have experienced misery, or hopelessness, or persons who have failed them, the Lord invites them: "Stop your crying, and wipe away your tears. You will be rewarded for your work, declares the Lord. You will return from the land of the enemy. Your future is filled with hope, declares, the Lord" (Jeremiah 31:16-17). God says, "At the right time I heard you. On the day of salvation I helped you. Listen, now is God's acceptable time! Now is the day of salvation!" (2 Corinthians 6:2). God welcomes each person to His family, the community of faith! The message is: "Come share in God's love and ours! Come share in His peace, strength, hope, and joy!"

Several years ago a pastor was asked to make a witnessing call to an inactive church family in the San Fernando Valley of California. He led them in a discussion of the family's relationship to Jesus Christ and what it means. After a short discussion with the teenage boy who had joined them, the pastor asked what the boy wanted to share. He said, "Well, I didn't like the letter I got from my church a few months ago, telling me I would be kicked out if I didn't attend church." This congregation, based on the letter, tended to emphasize church attendance more than a relationship to Jesus Christ.

Much welcomed by the family, the visit lasted about two hours. It centered on relevant questions that related their relationship with Christ to individual interests and concerns. When the pastor left, the father said, "Thanks for coming, and please come again soon. This is the first time in eighteen years that our family has had a discussion about our relationship with Jesus Christ." Sadly, many churches are concerned only about "churchianity," that members go to church. Church leaders should rather be leading families in discussions concerning their relationship with Christ, their Christianity.

At some time during a visit with inactive members, the shepherd may want to ask how the church may serve them. Shepherds may share questions and thoughts like this: "Have we in any way failed to serve and care for you? What can we do to meet your spiritual needs? How can we better pay attention to your concerns?"

If any members do not respond positively, they might be asked whether they want to be under the spiritual care of another church. If they want to continue membership, however, the shepherd should offer to help them become involved in small groups or fellowship activities with other members. If the answer is negative, the shepherd should agree with their decision and end with prayer.

Reclaiming and winning back members takes hard work—feeding, watering, and cultivating—before the seed grows to become a healthy plant. The congregation must recognize whether it has the strength and spiritual climate to give adequate nourishment and care to all weak and inactive members. Churches must be healthy and provide an atmosphere in which God's grace is freely available to inactive members.

The gospel can infuse the spiritual climate of the church with grace, inviting repentance, forgiveness, and reconciliation. The forgiving Word possesses power and strength. It is a unique, transforming grace in Christ. The experience of forgiveness from God is new assurance that He is working out His loving purpose in believers' lives.

THE OLD STONE CHURCH

Expressing the gospel in repentance, forgiveness, and reconciliation brings dramatic results. The story *Old Stone Church* by E.B. Hill[3] is especially touching:

> For five years my wife and I had been hearing about the Old Stone Church. We were told that it was a growing congregation with an effective Sunday school, and supported two full-time workers in Costa Rica.

The reputation that spread the farthest and seemed most remarkable, however, concerned the kind of caring fellowship the church had among members as diverse as recovered drug addicts, bank presidents, former prostitutes, farmers, ex-convicts, school teachers, and what-have-you.

I related this at a board meeting one night and got some typical reactions. George Hathaway said, "I'd hate to try to run a church with some of those members. You'd never know when they'd go back to their old habits and disgrace the congregation."

"Right," Jim Peoples agreed. "And that bit about supporting missionaries doesn't stir me much. I happen to know that's a paper mill town. All you'd need would be a couple of these big shots in a church to make that extra giving possible."

Guy Forbes spoke up: "Yes, and all that stuff about having so much love and caring sounds more like publicity than reality. Of course, it's more than a hundred miles from here. Maybe you'd find as much bickering and fault-finding there as, well, maybe even more than we have."

That was when I decided to visit the Old Stone Church when my family went to visit my folks in the fall. It wouldn't be far out of our way, and maybe it would answer some questions.

Funny thing was that when we finally got there we couldn't find the church. We'd planned to make it for the 11:00 a.m. worship, but by 11:10 we were still driving around looking. Surely in a town of this size you ought to be able to spot a big, old, stone church.

We finally got directions from a boy on a bicycle who pointed confidently at a fairly new red brick church. Since we were already late, we decided to worship there and find the other church later.

We sure were surprised to be handed a bulletin with the words on the cover welcoming us to Old Stone Church. After we were seated we noticed the picture on the bulletin. It was strange. A cross lay at a peculiar angle on a broken wooden surface.

My wife nudged me, and I looked where her eyes directed me. Sure enough, there in the front of the church was the real thing. It looked as if the heavy cross had dropped on to a beautiful walnut table and damaged it badly.

I must admit I'd had enough surprises, so I didn't hear much of the message that morning.

We lagged behind after the service. I wanted to know about the accident that had caused the cross to fall.

"Must have just happened, did it?" I asked an usher.

"Oh, no sir," he answered quickly. "It was when we first moved into this new church five years ago. It was the very first Sunday, in fact."

When the preacher greeted us, I hung on to his hand as if he might get away. "I need some information," I said. "This is all very confusing. Why is this new brick church called Old Stone Church, and why hasn't somebody done something about that fallen cross in five years?"

We were answered by a smile that told us he'd heard this before. He asked us if we had time to talk after the others left. We did, and he ushered us into his study.

I always talk too much, so I started out, "I suppose the 'Old Stone Church' name came from the fact that the old church was stone, and you just kept the name when you built this one."

"No," the preacher answered, "When I came, the congregation had an old white frame building. They were not much alive spiritually and the big push was to build a new building. That seemed to be the answer, they thought, to new life in the church."

"What happened?" I asked.

"Well, it's nothing to brag about," the preacher answered. "From the beginning we had unbelievable arguments. The spiteful things that were said and done almost drove me out of the ministry. We couldn't agree on anything. When the majority ruled, the minority threatened to withdraw support."

"For two years people fought with the architect and with one another. Some parts of the church had to be redesigned five times. Then at last we got down to the matter of a cross. Some old-timers said the one planned would make the church look Catholic. Others said all new Protestant churches were using crosses now."

"At last, they got to the place where they decided on a plain, heavy cross to be suspended over a handsome, polished walnut table. Most thought it was simple and tasteful, and for a day or two everything was reasonably peaceful. Then came a new explosion. How should the cross be suspended? The man who was donating it thought it should be held in place by a pipe extending from the wall to the point of intersection on the cross."

"Sounds reasonable," I commented, "but it wasn't done that way, was it?"

"No," the preacher answered. "That argument got so hot the donor of the cross left the church. He had been called bossy and self-centered for two years, but now somebody dug up an old indiscretion from his younger days and flung it at him just for spite. Then they suspended the cross from the ceiling with almost invisible nylon cords. The architect advised against it, talking about stress and strain. But it was to no avail."

"Well, during the first service the cross fell. It was a shocking thing to see and hear. Since nobody seemed to be in a worshipful mood anyway, bedlam broke loose. Everybody was blaming somebody else for all the things that had gone wrong during the building."

The preacher shook his head and then went on. "I was sure this would be my last service. I had failed to help them become a church. As one last act there I shouted for them to return to their seats. Reluctantly they did, except for old Brother Weaver who slipped out the door."

"I started to speak after most of the noise subsided. 'Look at the cross,' I said. 'We are not worthy to have it in our midst. As we look at it, let it speak to us of our sins, committed against one another and against the Lord. Just sit there and look at it!' They did, and for twenty minutes there was silence except for some low sobbing and much blowing of noses."

"While I looked at the cross myself, I decided it should stay just where it was. I knew I'd be staying, too.

"Then one man got up and quietly made his way toward another whom he had accused of terrible things. He asked for forgiveness, and they embraced. Soon just about everybody was following the example.

"After a while I called them to order again by singing 'Blest be the tie that binds our hearts in Christian love!'

"Just as we finished singing we heard a rumbling noise, and there, coming down the aisle was old Brother Weaver pulling a child's red wagon full of stones. When he got to the front of the church, he made a simple speech that went something like this:

'I went out and picked up these stones, and I want each of you to have one. Don't ever get rid of it until you're sure you should use it. Carry it with you every place you go. Whenever you get angry and want to hurt somebody, take that stone in your hand. While you squeeze it, remember the words of our Lord, 'He that is without sin among you, let him be first to cast a stone.' These are just plain old stones, but any old stone will do when you feel qualified to give it to one of God's children."

"Everybody took a stone and went home. If you had looked into pockets and purses here today you would have found that we all had stones with us. And we present our new members with stones and tell them the story. Those little old stones have been used of the Lord to transform this church!"

The preacher had finished, and it was time for us to go.

"I'm thrilled with what I've heard here today," I said, as I extended my hand toward the preacher. "You are to be congratulated. This church was dying, I understand, when you took over. Of course, I have heard that the preacher ahead of you couldn't preach worth a cent, and he certainly wasn't an organizer, and…"

The preacher's look stopped me. Without taking his eyes off me, he reached over and handed me a stone. I stared at it. And then I understood the significance of the revival in the Old Stone Church. I carry that stone with me everywhere I go even though, as Brother Weaver said, any old stone would do.

This descriptive narrative shows the kind of repentance, forgiveness, and reconciliation every healthy church must have! In a worship service, a pastor read this story and shared stones with the worshipers. It was a dramatic experience as the participants were encouraged to practice what they had just heard. This message can be shared in churches so they experience a more healthy culture and be spiritually renewed.

Judson Cornwall writes: "Repentance should be as common to the Christian as breathing. We exhale the bad and inhale the good. We will breathe out repentance and breathe in forgiveness. We will rid ourselves of inward sin and receive as the reverse and subsequent action, the righteousness of God." When this happens, forgiveness follows. Forgiveness restores and keeps believers in a living relationship with God. It gives inner healing and provides the strength to daily glorify God.

Cornwall goes on to say, "Let us enjoy forgiveness. We have been restored to a whole new life. Let's live it…We have been justified; let's enjoy it. In Christ we have been sanctified; let's savor it to the fullest. We are being glorified; let's delight in it. Let's stop listening to our memory circuits, and reprogram our minds to enjoy our new status as forgiven and loved people. Rejoice! Sing! Shout! God's love has triumphed over His law. Enjoy it! Let's enjoy forgiveness!"[4]

Nurturing congregations today should have small groups, as did the early church.

Members need to gather for Bible study, extending mutual support that is centered on the Word. The seed-planting church, nurturing church is to be a place of healing and love, a place where the Holy Spirit binds up the broken hearted. It needs to find new and meaningful ways to consistently show unconditional love. Those in need must be sought out. Ministries of listening, mutual support, connecting, and prayer, need to be readily accessible to members and their neighbors.

Hurting people in the church need to experience the love of God. They need to experience the incarnational ministries of compassionate listening and caring presence. They must be shown grace and forgiveness. The seed-planting, nurturing church cares for the entire field, including those persons who have been inactive. It has a passion to bring all persons to a vibrant, living relationship with Jesus that is evidenced in growing, healthy relationships with His people. All together will celebrate with joy as many are touched with the healing and restoration of God's love.

Can you take a moment to picture a scene of a Kansas sunflower farm in all its beauty and symmetry of blooming heads atop the green, verdant plants. A neighbor's sunflower field in contrast differs with about 40% of the plants being healthy and about 60% sickly with drooping, pale leaves with no blossoms. How long will church leaders of traditional churches which resemble the latter picture endure and allow such circumstances under the Headship of Christ? **The Seed-Planting Church** faces this scenario directly as it opens the scriptures to review what the grace of God can and does accomplish through faithful leaders of the church. What does this chapter offer to correct this situation in congregations? The supernatural love of God!

CHAPTER 7

Healthy Churches Use Quality Control Systems

Factories and businesses use them for good production. Farmer Jim uses them for healthy productivity. Both employ quality control systems for designing and monitoring their businesses for better yield. In the same way, those who understand the teachings of Jesus and Paul know they are applying a biblical strategy and quality control system in their churches.

In order to employ a biblical quality control system, a "monitor" (one that recognizes whether the church is utilizing an effective strategy) needs to be developed and adopted. This monitor detects whether the church is pursuing the right path toward health. A quality control system or "guide" becomes the tool that oversees and accomplishes the equipping strategy in the church.

There are at least three available tools that can serve as quality control systems for churches today. One is *Natural Church Development* by Christian Schwarz[1]. This tool measures the effective characteristics of a church. Related to this, *12 Pillars of a Healthy Church*[2] provides a quality strategic system for guiding congregations in building healthy characteristics and monitoring them for quality control. Together, *Natural Church Development* and *12 Pillars of a Healthy Church* offer a new equation and framework that proposes biblical principles to replace traditional programmatic, harvesting paradigms. Rick Warren offers a third strategic system in *The Purpose Driven Church*[3]. He demonstrates in his book how members can be purposefully guided from membership to maturity to ministry to mission.

NATURAL CHURCH DEVELOPMENT

Christian Schwarz offers a most natural biblical approach as he applies growth concepts of nature to the church. Laws of organic growth look at the roots and health of a plant, not just at the fruit. Harvesting churches characteristically look only for fruit seen on the surface. Schwarz points out, "See the lilies of the field, *how they grow*" (Matthew 6:18). Churches must intensely and diligently learn, observe, study, and research this growth. He emphasizes the *growth mechanisms*, not the beauty of the lilies. This is important in understanding the principles of kingdom work.

Natural Church Development stresses principles of biological growth. God has created all living organisms with the capacity to grow and reproduce "automatically." It is a natural process. These natural principles also apply to the body of Christ and the Christian community of faith. Jesus had used many illustrations from nature to describe the kingdom of God. Schwarz says leaders can learn from all forms of life and transfer those concepts to the living organism called the Church.

Schwarz developed these natural principles from three sources: (1) empirical research, (2) observation of nature, and (3) the study of scripture. He notes that natural church development does not attempt to "make" a church grow, but recognizes and releases the growth automatism with which God Himself builds the church. Schwarz contrasts the natural growth paradigm with the technocratic. In the technocratic, the significance of institutions, programs, and methods is overestimated, while in spiritual growth, their significance is underestimated.

Schwarz divides his book into five sections. The first four sections represent the four building blocks of natural church development. (1) Content: what needs to be done—*eight quality characteristics*, (2) Timing: when it should be done—*the minimum strategy*, (3) Method: how it should be done—*six biotic principles*, (4) Background: why it should be done—*the theological paradigm*.

The fifth section presents ten action steps for the practical implementation of the four building blocks. Leaders must (1) build spiritual momentum, (2) determine their minimum factors, (3) set qualitative goals, (4) identify obstacles, (5) apply biotic principles, (6) exercise their strengths, (7) utilize biotic tools, (8) monitor effectiveness, (9) address their new minimum factors, and (10) multiply their church.

All five sections of the book provide a foundation for the building of an effective strategy, a quality control system, for the church. Breakthrough leaders need to become familiar with the *Natural Church Development* strategy and its quality control system of eight characteristics. Schwarz's research is based on a cross-sampling of one thousand churches in thirty-two countries. The churches used for the research were large and small, growing and declining, persecuted and state-subsidized, charismatic and non-charismatic, prominent models and unknown churches. The study of 4.2 million responses was an attempt to give a scientifically based answer to the question, "What is a healthy church?"

In his years of thorough research, Schwarz has identified the link between church health and growth by looking at the eight essential elements of health in churches. These quality characteristics are (1) empowering leadership, (2) gift-oriented ministry, (3) passionate spirituality, (4) functional structures, (5) inspiring worship services, (6) holistic small groups, (7) need-centered evangelism, and (8) loving relationships.

According to Schwarz, no church that wants to grow qualitatively and quantitatively can afford to overlook any one of these quality characteristics.[4] He says that, in evaluating health, a healthy church "must have attained a quality index of sixty-five in all eight areas," at minimum. His research showed that no one single factor leads to growth in churches. Rather, it is the interplay of all eight elements. No one element can be absolutized at the expense of all others. He writes, "There is one rule for which we did not find a single exception among the churches surveyed. Every church that reached a quality index of sixty-five or more (for each of the eight quality characteristics) is a growing church. *This is perhaps the most spectacular discovery of our survey.*"[5]

Schwarz learned that there is a qualitative difference between growing and declining churches. Growing churches have a higher quality index in all eight areas than declining ones. "The 'sixty-five hypothesis' states that whenever all eight values climb to 65, the statistical probability that the church is growing is 99.4%. Again, this is one of the few church growth principles for which we have yet to find a single exception anywhere in the world."[6]

A survey for Natural Church Development is also available.[7] With this survey, the congregation learns reliable, validated, objective "hard data" from which to make a prescription for health. It is based on a "principle-oriented" approach rather than that of a model. Churches using the survey receive individualized help, not general observations or a "one-size-fits-all" model. A worldwide standard of measurement is the measuring tool in the congregation. Critical factors that keep the church from increased health and growth are identified. The same survey and database can monitor the effectiveness year after year. The healthier the church, the more it grows and multiplies.

12 PILLARS OF A HEALTHY CHURCH

12 Pillars of a Healthy Church[8] offers two approaches, that of the twelve pillars (the eight quality characteristics and four additional leading indicators of healthy churches) and that of the ball-field (Rick Warren's illustration in *The Purpose Driven Church*).

Added to the eight fore-mentioned quality characteristics are four additional leading indicators of healthy churches: (9) the centrality of God's Word, the gospel, and grace, (10) the fact that a church must be mission and vision driven, (11) the truth of biblical financial stewardship, and (12) the commitment to church planting.

These stress the 2 Timothy discipling model of life-giving churches. They result in a balance of inreach and outreach.

Each characteristic in *12 Pillars of a Healthy Church* includes a "Reality Check" that allows leaders and members to measure or assess the strengths and weaknesses of the congregation. A practical facet of the book is the proposal for "Maximum and Minimum Level Activities" for each characteristic. These are all based on biblical references and insights. Also included is a helpful listing of primary and secondary resources, books that are vital for a better understanding of the issues.

Local congregations are living organisms, created and designed by God to grow and reproduce. Churches grown according to these strategies are positioned to engage in ministry that births new life. To revitalize a congregation, God first transforms the lives of the pastor and church leaders. These in turn create, by God's power, new biblical strategies that produce more and stronger disciples. A church life system is created based upon biblical belief.

The twelve basic pillars are the life system or process that grows out of the Word of life. Each of the twelve pillars of a healthy church interacts with the others to increase the capacity for ministry impact. They help a church to restructure and revitalize its established style, structure, and strategy. Isaiah 43:18-19 states a principle relevant for this process: "Forget what happened in the past, and do not dwell on events from long ago. I am going to do something new. It is already happening. Don't you recognize it?"

Leading a congregation to introduce the twelve pillars of a healthy church is best done when a series of sermons and Bible studies, based on each of the twelve pillars, are scheduled. Some churches have offered them only as special Bible studies, but there is great benefit in scheduling the sermons to coincide with the timing of the studies. These sermons and studies can be scheduled as a four or six week series, depending upon available time. Sample sermons and Bible studies titled *The Health Church-Sermons and Bible Studies* are available from Concordia University.[9]

The approach of the twelve pillars is that of a ministry of transformation, not a ministry of new programs. Introducing layers of new and innovative procedures cannot change traditional systems. Neither can making mechanical or structural adjustments. These only meekly attempt to restructure the church. Such "changes" still retain mediocrity. The focus must be on a holistic strategy in which *God* transforms the church. It is only the Word and its "grace system" that can shape anything the church is able to do.

RICK WARREN'S "PURPOSE-DRIVEN CHURCH"

The third strategy, serving as a quality control system, is found in Rick Warren's book *The Purpose-Driven Church*.[10] His "ball-field illustration" is reproduced in *12 Pillars of a Healthy Church*. This diagram illustrates members, taken from the start of their relationship with the church, to bases one, two, three, and all the way "home."[11] Warren summarizes these stages as follows:

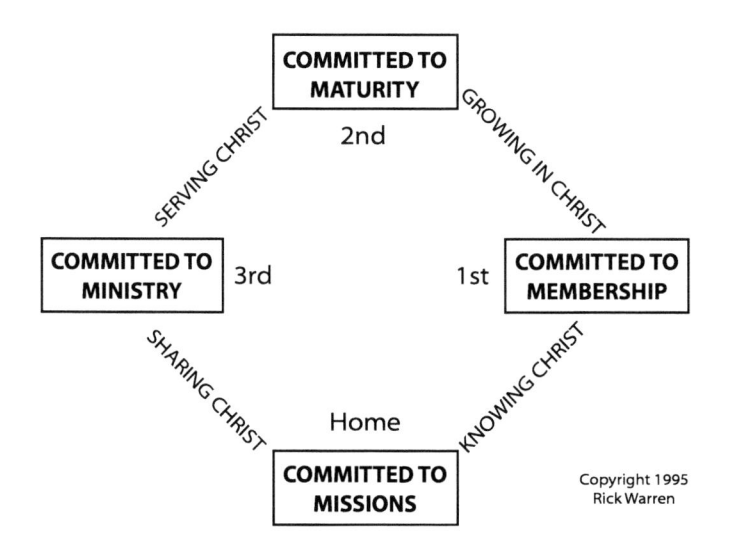

Base One represents the goal of bringing each member to know Christ. Some churches require very little for membership. It almost seems as if some persons are "carried" into the church or get there "limping." Far too many are listed as members when, in actuality, they have little or no commitment to the church. Some are merely "spectators" and participate only at Christmas and Easter. Some are close to first base, but just "hang around" it with no desire to go on to the next base. Joining a church should require basic study of Christian doctrine and faith. Full membership then includes living a life committed to Christ through consistent worship and Bible study. It involves actively participating in the ministry and mission of the church.

Base Two represents the goal of empowering each member to become mature. The focus is on the development of character, not mere knowledge or external behaviors and actions. In order for this maturity to develop, members must be in personal daily study of the Word. In addition, mentoring relationships are to be established and training given in areas of discipleship.

Base Three represents the goal of mobilizing each member for ministry. Members who have reached third base are to be fully committed to Christian service and servanthood. They are led to discover their spiritual gifts and to use them faithfully (Ephesians 4:7).

Home Base represents the goal of discipling each member to desire involvement in evangelism and missions. Believers who have "reached" home base are deeply convicted to share what Christ has done both for their salvation and personally in their lives.

12 Pillars of a Healthy Church (pages 90-105) provides a dynamic strategy that pastors and leaders of seed-planting, nurturing churches should review. It offers a simple visual planning grid for the church master plan as well as for individual ministries. The grid ("Christian Life Development Process for Members and Leaders—Moving from Membership to Mission, Transforming a Congregation to a Biblical Model," from *12 Pillars*, pg. 103) offers goals, resources, and leadership responsibilities not only for the four bases, but also as a pitcher's mound—leadership development—as follows.

The goals and resources of this ball-field graph have been developed for the empowering and mobilizing of God's people for mission. The goals and resources of each base have been summarized to give a quick overview of what this helpful nurturing strategy offers.

BASE ONE: INCORPORATE MEMBERS WHO KNOW AND CONFESS CHRIST

Members of a church need to be embraced and lovingly incorporated into the fold. They not only are to know and confess Christ, but also are to live for Him as active participants in the body of Christ. Part of their commitment as members is to receive relevant Bible-based instruction that establishes them in the Christian faith and places them into meaningful relationships with fellow believers. Reaching first base is the first step to a lifelong relationship with Christ and with fellow Christians.

Pastors and leaders of congregations have the responsibility for providing the rich soil in which individuals grow and are nourished for life. Incorporation or assimilation into the congregation, is important. This includes establishing membership standards, ones that echo the basic disciplines of the Christian faith. Weekly corporate worship, study of the scriptures, prayer, and participation in service and ministry opportunities are crucial for the spiritual formation of every member. All of these structures and activities build and foster relationships in the congregation's circle of care.

Institutional, harvesting churches place minimal expectations on their members. These low expectations are one of the direct reasons for poor church health. This is not acceptable. In fact, membership standards or requirements presently used by programmatic churches lead to religious mediocrity. Biblical standards for members' spirituality must be determined and expected. Failure to do so simply doesn't make sense.

Churches must educate their members and place expectations for growth. The curriculum for Christian growth and discipleship needs to be comprehensive in its scope. It should help God's people connect with Christ and with one another. Living triumphantly under the Cross and consistently in the Word results in faithful Christian service, ministry, and mission.

The environment in which the pastor, elders, deacons, and education leaders minister to members needs to be one in which all members can in return minister to each other. *12 Pillars of a Healthy Church* suggests a "Standard of Ten Biblical Expectations for Church Membership," which are expectations that help promote this type of environment. These should be carefully studied and considered for adaptation or adoption. In addition, the web site www.healthychurch.com provides information for lively interactive discipling courses like *Spiritual Travel Guide* and *21st Century Disciples with a 1st Century Faith*.

BASE TWO: EMPOWER MEMBERS TO SPIRITUAL MATURITY

Very few church members reach second base. Many go from a minimal first base of membership, bypass second, and go on to the third base of ministry and service. As a result, service and ministry involvement is exercised without spiritual maturity and an adequate understanding of God's Word. Members often do the work of ministry without the spiritual maturity to complete it effectively. All maturing members, however, will systematically be empowered in three areas: They are growing in Christ, are being discipled, and are becoming disciplers themselves.

Spiritual disciplines and prayer are to be taught. The study of God's Word is important for empowerment of members in the church. Mentoring relationships are to be established. Servant events and mission trips should be a part of the discipling and mentoring process. All these are not for mere knowledge or discipline. They are not merely to change external actions or behavior. The focus is on developing the inner life, making an internal change, focusing on heart and character, growing to maturity.

BASE THREE: ENLIST AND MOBILIZE MEMBERS TO SERVICE AND SERVANTHOOD

The nurturing church must be committed to placing members into ministry areas of giftedness. Believers that have been led to discover, and then use, their spiritual gifts in service to the church have reached third base. They are to be ministers of God's grace. They are to be caregivers that serve others in Christ's body, the church.

A church committed to ministry systematically leads all members to discover and use the spiritual gifts God has given them. Members are to recognize that they have been gifted to serve and that they are to be ministers of God's grace in every aspect of their lives. In addition, members are to be faithful stewards or managers of the financial resources God has given. They are also to be caregivers to persons in their circle—any family members, friends, neighbors, or church members—especially those who may be hurting.

HOME BASE: ENLIST AND MOBILIZE MEMBERS FOR WITNESSING AND MISSION OUTREACH

Members who are committed to evangelism and missions have reached home base. Evangelism and mission leaders in the nurturing church have provided a ministry of witnessing that leads members to effectively share the saving gospel with those in their sphere of influence. They emphasize and encourage members to build relationships and share the good news with those who are without Christ. All are challenged to go beyond their comfort zone and to be active in their own mission fields.

The goal is for believers to be messengers of God's love and to make Christ known. Mission education programs should be offered so that members are informed about world missions and encouraged to get involved in mission opportunities.

THE PITCHER'S MOUND—THE PROCESS ENABLER'S MOUND

Those on the pitcher's mound equip and mentor leaders that build a healthy church. Healthy leaders in healthy churches nurture healthy members. Empowering and mobilizing leaders is key. Leadership training begins with the pastor and then focuses on lay leaders. Empowerment gives all leaders, both pastors and lay persons, the training and the tools to use their grace-gifts as God directs. Empowerment gives them the strength to mobilize God's people for ministry and mission.

The pastor's leadership should not only empower but also release leaders for ministry. The pastoral function is to build a unified team of leaders who enable a full-bodied fellowship of believers. Teaching and training is important at all levels of membership, but it is crucial that all who assume leadership positions are active in Bible study and leadership development. Nurturing congregations will adopt policies that insure such criteria. A transition time of several years should be planned for leaders who have not participated in these in the past.

Healthy churches emphasize disciple-making as a spiritual dynamic. Leaders, those on the pitcher's mound, are key to this disciple-making. These leaders must encourage a Great Commission lifestyle, the type of lives that count now and for eternity. Breakthrough leaders in healthy churches know that their influence, based on the example of Christ and His almighty Word, is crucial. The influence of these breakthrough leaders is far more important than control. Their influence and their example encourages members to live "by faith in the Son of God who gave Himself up" for them (Galatians 2:20).

THE DEVELOPMENT OF A SEED-PLANTING, NURTURING VISION

Each chapter presented in this book contributes to the development of a church that plants seeds and nurtures its members. A biblical vision is presented of how congregations can be healthy and rid themselves of negative harvesting components. These principles constitute the vision for reaching and nourishing every member of the congregation.

This book, together with the books *Natural Church Development* and *12 Pillars of a Healthy Church*, should be read and studied for direction. They outline the necessary components for growing a biblical church that plants seeds and nurtures its members. A vision task force or leadership group should be enlisted to discern and develop the vision for the ministry. This task force should include the pastor, church chairperson, and representatives of each ministry group, board, or committee. It should also include several potential leaders, both men and women, gifted in leadership. Each person on this task force should read these three books.

George Barna gave this widely used and accepted definition of vision: "Vision for ministry is a clear mental image of a preferable future imparted by God to His chosen servants and is based upon an accurate understanding of God, self, and circumstances." This type of vision can assist the church to discern and develop its strategy. It can lead them to seed-planting, nurturing activities. It can help them stay on track as it works toward reaching its biblical purpose. A church that defines its vision and adopts a vision statement experiences many benefits and blessings. A vision:

- Gives assurance that the church is doing God's work, not busy work
- Provides encouragement and the intensity to pursue a strategy
- Gives the church an overall direction
- Defines what the church should and should not do
- Provides a basis for measuring what is done
- Encourages accountability
- Unifies members in a common goal

DISCERNING, DEVELOPING, AND APPLYING THE VISION

The process of discerning the vision might begin with a series of sermons and Bible studies on the *12 Pillars of a Healthy Church*. Each week worshipers might be given a sheet of paper to answer the following questions (regarding each of the twelve pillars):

1. In your view, how are we doing in this area?

2. Where do you believe God wants us to go?
3. What strengths do you see in our congregation in this area?
4. What weaknesses do you see in our congregation in this area?
5. What advances would you like to see us make?
6. What insights can you offer for growth in this area?

In order to discern the vision, sufficient time must be allowed for persons to respond with their reflections and insights. The significant responses from those answering the above questions should then be recorded. A group should study these responses and begin to develop the church's unique vision.

Vision leaders should allow one year for such studies and responses. During this time, any barriers to health can be recognized and identified. New strength can be gained, new direction taken—a new determination to follow God and His Word. The church can recommit and revision to "Catch the Vision of Christ's Mission."

During this year of visioning, the Word needs to be richly sowed. It is the Word that produces results. Over time, more persons will grow to be disciples: "The churches were being strengthened in the faith, and grew in numbers every day" (Acts 16:5).

HAVING A VISION LEADS TO DEVELOPING A MASTER MINISTRY STRATEGY

As the vision is developed, a clearer direction comes into focus. The vision becomes the basis for a master ministry strategy. In order to develop this strategy, the vision task force must take the newly-formed vision to each individual ministry board and group in the congregation. Each group must connect their particular ministry responsibility to the church vision. In order to be adequately informed in the process, group members should be encouraged to read the resource books. This will enable them better to be prepared to develop the vision into a master vision strategy. By the end of the first year, this master ministry strategy should be completed. If a church is committed to determining its purpose and vision, it must be intentional in planning its strategy. In order to plan this ministry strategy, each group should ask the questions, "What do we think God is calling our church to be and do?" "How will we do what He has asked us to do?" "How can we be what we believe He is asking us to be?" Steps in developing this master ministry strategy involve:

- analysis (where the church is now)
- understanding the situation (the statistics)
- vision (what God wants our church to be)
- goals (what the ministries of the church should be)
- programs (how the church moves ahead with its strategies)
- evaluation (making sure that we pursue and complete the ministry strategy)

Strategic planning is an investment, not merely an expenditure of time. It requires careful attention to immediate needs and choices. An effective plan or strategy will be specific and detailed. It requires commitment on the part of all participants in the planning process. Effective planning demands that the efforts be commensurate to the vital ministries that need to be accomplished. Short-term advances should be generated as well as long-term results. The seed-planting and nurturing vision must be anchored in the strategy and must result in broad-based action.

It would be helpful to develop a forum where church members can discuss their place in the "priesthood of all believers." Questions can be asked that encourage members to evaluate this position personally and corporately. "What is your purpose in life?" "Why do you think God placed you here on earth?" "Why do you think God placed you in this church at this time?" "How can our church be biblical in its ministries?"

Planning instruments from *12 Pillars of a Healthy Church* (the Rick Warren ball-field grid and the two forms on pages 117-118) help the leaders to take necessary steps toward transforming the church to be what God wants it to be. The development of a ministry strategy will give deep sense of meaning and purpose to the daily activities of leaders. It will help them to periodically evaluate the thrust of their work and to determine the quality of their efforts.

CHAPTER 7

CHRISTIAN LIFE DEVELOPMENT PROCESS FOR MEMBERS AND LEADERS MOVING FROM MEMBERSHIP TO MISSIONS
Transforming a Congregation to a Biblical Model

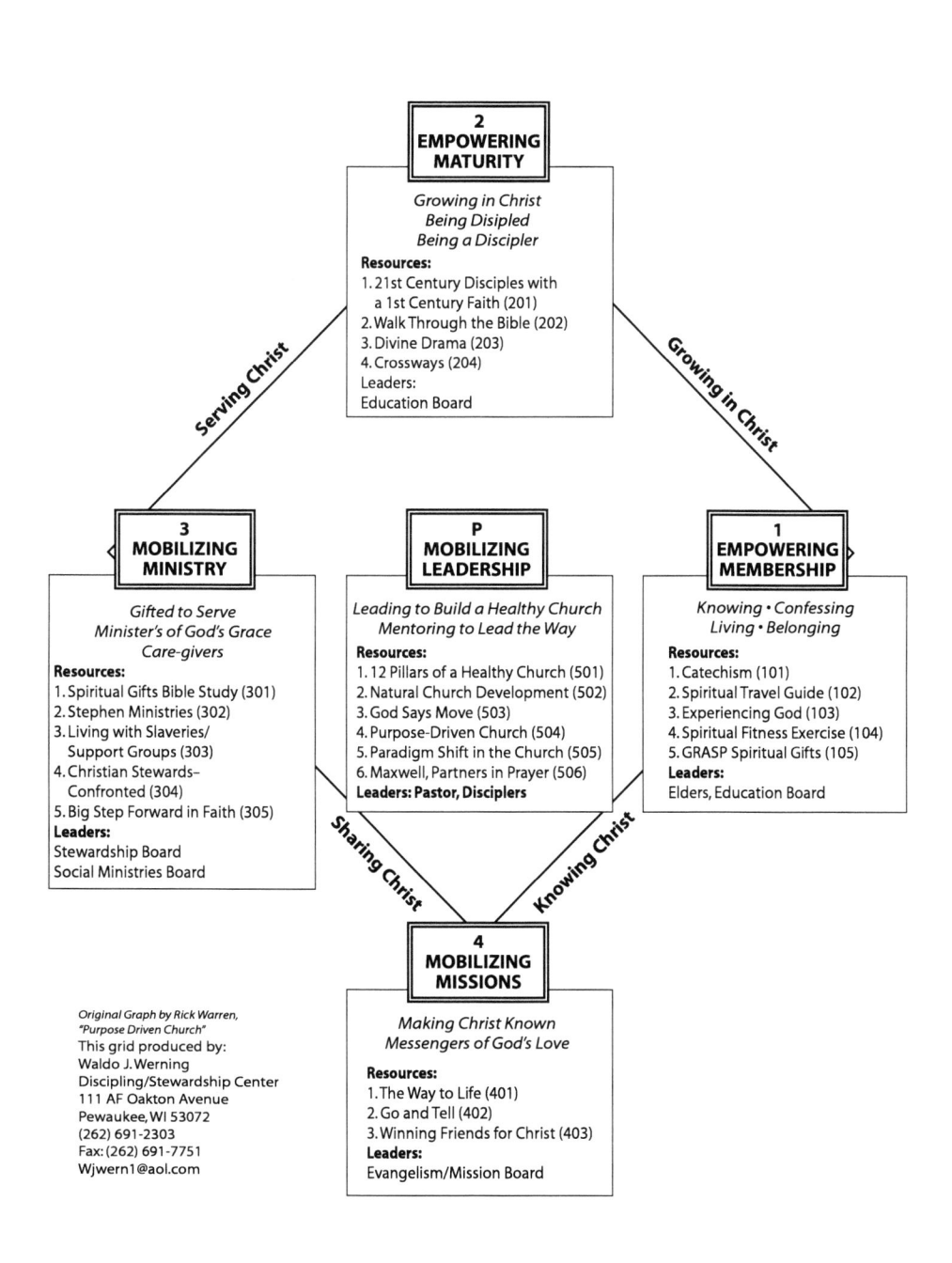

2 EMPOWERING MATURITY

Growing in Christ
Being Disipled
Being a Discipler

Resources:
1. 21st Century Disciples with a 1st Century Faith (201)
2. Walk Through the Bible (202)
3. Divine Drama (203)
4. Crossways (204)

Leaders:
Education Board

Serving Christ — *Growing in Christ*

3 MOBILIZING MINISTRY

Gifted to Serve
Minister's of God's Grace
Care-givers

Resources:
1. Spiritual Gifts Bible Study (301)
2. Stephen Ministries (302)
3. Living with Slaveries/ Support Groups (303)
4. Christian Stewards–Confronted (304)
5. Big Step Forward in Faith (305)

Leaders:
Stewardship Board
Social Ministries Board

P MOBILIZING LEADERSHIP

Leading to Build a Healthy Church
Mentoring to Lead the Way

Resources:
1. 12 Pillars of a Healthy Church (501)
2. Natural Church Development (502)
3. God Says Move (503)
4. Purpose-Driven Church (504)
5. Paradigm Shift in the Church (505)
6. Maxwell, Partners in Prayer (506)

Leaders: Pastor, Disciplers

1 EMPOWERING MEMBERSHIP

Knowing • Confessing
Living • Belonging

Resources:
1. Catechism (101)
2. Spiritual Travel Guide (102)
3. Experiencing God (103)
4. Spiritual Fitness Exercise (104)
5. GRASP Spiritual Gifts (105)

Leaders:
Elders, Education Board

Sharing Christ — *Knowing Christ*

4 MOBILIZING MISSIONS

Making Christ Known
Messengers of God's Love

Resources:
1. The Way to Life (401)
2. Go and Tell (402)
3. Winning Friends for Christ (403)

Leaders:
Evangelism/Mission Board

Original Graph by Rick Warren, "Purpose Driven Church"
This grid produced by:
Waldo J. Werning
Discipling/Stewardship Center
111 AF Oakton Avenue
Pewaukee, WI 53072
(262) 691-2303
Fax: (262) 691-7751
Wjwern1@aol.com

APPLYING THE VISION AND THE MASTER MISSION STRATEGY—A THREE-YEAR PROCESS

When the vision and master mission strategy is completed—approximately one year into the process—the vision task force must motivate every ministry board and group in the congregation to activate productive ministry in their respective areas. This needs to be fully on the basis of the vision of Christ's mission. The "Apply the Vision" activity is a three-year process. The pastor and vision leaders begin by educating the entire congregation through dynamic messages and attractive printed materials. The vision and master mission strategy should be duplicated and available for all members. The mission strategy with the grid is now the "map" that all leaders follow in applying the strategy to each specific area of ministry. It is crucial that fervent prayer undergird the entire effort. In order to meet ministry goals, all possible resources are to be used. In addition, leaders must be held accountable for targeting every individual of the congregation. Vision leaders should keep asking relevant questions:

- Have we reviewed long-standing methods, programs, and decisions to learn if they are still valid on the basis of biblical principles?
- Have we looked at all alternatives?
- Have we set the proper priorities?
- Do we see an opportunity in every difficulty or crisis?
- Do we face and make difficult decisions head-on?
- Are we keeping the main thing the main thing?
- Have we distinguished between constants and variables?
- Have the vision committee leaders and church board leaders done their homework by reading the three basic resource books?

As the master mission strategy is produced and finalized, leaders will want to study carefully the "Personal Discipleship Inventory" developed by Gloria Dei Lutheran Church, Houston, Texas.[12] Appendix A displays the "Personal Discipleship Inventory" which requests a thoughtful personal evaluation and commitment in the areas of lifestyle, witness, prayer, care, spiritual gifts, finance and stewardship. Encouraging the members to become fully devoted followers of Jesus as a life-long pursuit, each disciple then is asked to develop their own "personal discipleship plan."

You will see that every member is assigned in a support group under the care of a Lay Minister or Assistant Lay Minister. Leaders will do well to develop their own Personal Discipleship Inventory for their congregation.

THE DEFINING MOMENT

There are defining moments in the life of the church. Transforming a church from a harvesting church to a seed-planting church is not merely a defining moment, but *the* defining moment in the entire history of a congregation. Church leaders can discern the vision—and even develop a general plan—but still fail to adopt a master mission strategy that can be aggressively introduced to church members. The defining moment of transformation pierces to the very heart of the life and reality of the congregation.

Assuming that the spiritual leaders and task force group have adopted a master mission strategy, the *defining moment* becomes reality when steps are taken to *apply the vision* during a three-year process. When this is done, all the criticisms, excuses, and defenses of the previous maintenance and programmatic experiences have been set aside. The choices, events, and people once enslaved to institutional, harvesting forms and functions are history. The Holy Spirit is able to give spiritual leaders a clear vision in this defining moment. They know how they will aggressively apply the seed-planting strategy biblically and practically.

The apostle Paul spoke of the sacred responsibility laid upon church leaders. He said they are entrusted with the gospel. The Savior Himself spoke of working "while it is day" before night comes, "when no one can do anything," when opportunities are gone (John 9:4). God has called His people to the ministry of accepting the vision of Christ's mission, of discerning and developing it, and of applying it in the church.

Many years ago, veteran missionary Lillian Dickson in Taiwan faced demands from every side. Depressed, she broke into tears saying, "I just can't meet all these mission demands!" A voice seemed to whisper, "*Who* can't?" Missionary Dickson recalled, "I was stunned by such a thought. Did I presume to think it was I who had this mission burden by myself? Would I dare to say what the *Lord* can't do?" Despite people and circumstances who tried to slow her down, Lillian Dickson went on to build mission bridges over chasms, handling mission crises and opportunities as she met them. Her mission policy was, "Where there's a need, fill it! You can have a conference later—on how it was done!"

Leaders must ask themselves the questions: "Do I hear the call to service as a vision-leader to stand before the congregation?" "Can I wholeheartedly affirm the sovereignty of God as well as His love and mercy?" "Can I transpose God's goodness and faithfulness onto the process of building a healthy church with twelve quality characteristics and pillars?" "Do I as a church leader see beyond pews, pulpits, altars, programs, positions, meetings and traditions (maintenance concerns)?" "Can I see this church as a healthy seed-planting, nurturing church?" God will complete any mission when He Himself wants it done. Strategies that have been prayerfully planned and guided by the Holy Spirit will be completed in His timing and in His way.

Vision leaders will let the seed-planting and nurturing principles be enlarged and deepened throughout the ministries of the church. Every man, woman, and child needs to hear what the Spirit is saying to the Church. Let the gospel trumpet of Christ's vision of His mission be heard—so every church will be a healthy church!

CHAPTER 8

Leaders with Faith that Produces Character and a Heart Like God

Good leaders—those with character and heart—make a difference. Dilbert, of the newspaper comics, articulates an idea that lends some thoughts on the subject.[1] Dilbert confides, "Both plans are technically impossible." "Which one costs less?" his manager asks. "Um…I don't see how that matters," Dilbert replies, "but Plan One is much cheaper."

The manager goes to his supervisor and reports, "Plan One is best." "I'll take it to the VP," the supervisor says. Well, the VP views the selections and responds, "I like Plan Two." "Great minds think alike…" replies the supervisor. "Excellent! Ask one of our engineers to present Plan Two to the board." The manager turns to Dilbert and says, "Guess what." Dilbert comes to the conclusion, "Everyday I make the world a little bit worse." "What's it like," the supervisor responds, "to make a difference?"

Spiritual leaders with strong character and a heart like God make a big difference! How does a person develop that kind of character, that kind of heart? The simple answer—faith! The author of the book of Hebrews described the gift of faith: "Faith assures us of things we expect and convinces us of the existence of things we cannot see" (Hebrews 11:1). Those who showed great faith in Hebrews 11 made a difference! Spiritual leaders in the congregation likewise can make the difference between church mediocrity and church health, between a harvesting congregation and a seed-planting congregation. "No one can please God without faith," the writer goes on. "Whoever goes to God must believe that God exists and that He rewards those who seek Him" (11:6). The leader who wants to please God must have faith! God seeks for leaders after His own heart. Those are the types of leaders He chooses to appoint. They are leaders with faith, leaders who *believe* Him and act accordingly! They are leaders who seek Him wholeheartedly.

David had a heart like God's.[2] Samuel told Saul that "the Lord has searched for a man after His own heart. The Lord has appointed him leader of His people" (1 Samuel 13:14). Samuel was speaking about the young man David. David's heart and his character made a difference as he led the people. His heart and character flowed out of His deep faith in an almighty, all-powerful, ever-loving God. Leaders must develop a deep faith that produces character and heart.

1. Faith-full leaders will experience battles and encounter "giants."

In any congregation, leaders must face battles—financial battles, relational battles, any number of other battles. The nature of the battle can vary from fairly simple circumstances to those that seem humanly impossible to face. Some battles threaten to discourage leaders in the church. The fact remains; leaders know battles happen. They *will* face giants.

In 1 Samuel 17 relates a battle between Israel and the Philistines. The Philistine army's champion was the ten-foot-tall Goliath. "Choose a man," Goliath yelled, "and let him come down to fight me…I challenge the Israelite battle line today" (1 Samuel 17:1-10). The scene was familiar in those days. Enemies arose and battles happened.

But this giant was different. His armor weighed 125 pounds, his spear point 15 pounds—a total of 140 pounds. That is no different than carrying a healthy 15-year-old son on one's back! No wonder Israel was fearful! Scripture says Saul and all the Israelites "were gripped with fear" (v. 11). "When all the men of Israel saw Goliath, they fled from him because they were terrified" (v. 24). Israel was paralyzed with fear.

However, a spiritual leader was to call God's people back to faith. God had told Israel, "Before the battle starts, have a priest come and speak to your troops. He should tell them, 'Listen, Israel, today you're going into battle against your enemies. Don't lose your courage! Don't be afraid or be alarmed or tremble because of them. The Lord your God is going with you. He will fight for you against your enemies and give you victory'" (Deuteronomy 20:2-4). God's words in Deuteronomy had directed Israel to ordain a leader to remind the nation of His promise. Saul, Israel's chosen one, forgot that promise. This leader looked with human eyes instead of with eyes focused on the Almighty God and His promise. Lack of faith led an entire army into faithlessness. Leaders cannot afford to listen to giants. If they do, fears will take over their territory, take over their thoughts, and make them think they have no power! God requires faith.

2. Faith-full leaders understand the nature of the battle.

David knew the nature of the battle! "You come to me with sword and spear and javelin, but I come to you in the name of the Lord of armies, the God of the army of Israel, whom you have insulted," David told the Philistine. "Today the Lord will hand you over to me. I will strike you down...The whole world will know that Israel has a God" (I Samuel 17:45-46). David knew this battle was a spiritual battle.

Leaders and churches participate in a spiritual battle. "This is not a wrestling match against a human opponent. We are wrestling with...the powers who govern this world of darkness, and spiritual forces that control evil..." (Ephesians 6:12). Churches can give in and settle into earthly molds, or they can go against the tide and follow God's way. Leaders with God's heart know the "battle" is all about God's glory. The battle is a spiritual battle and God's honor is at stake.

"Who is this uncircumcised Philistine that he should challenge the army of *the living God?*" David asked (I Samuel 17: 26). "No one should be discouraged because of this," he told Saul. "I will go and fight this Philistine" (v. 32). David knew God. He knew the battle was *His*. Leaders, though they experience real circumstances in the visible, physical realm, know that the battle is spiritual. They must understand its nature, and that it is God's. A leader must see the battle through eyes of faith, not through human eyes and emotions. The outcome is for *God's* glory.

3. Faith-full leaders remember past victories.

"The Lord, who saved me from the lion and the bear, will save me from this Philistine" (v. 37), David recalled. He knew that the God who had worked in the past was able to help Israel now. In contrast, Israel's army saw a large man. God's people became so afraid that they turned around and ran! This demonstrated lack of faith

God had told Israel, "You may say to yourselves, 'These nations outnumber us.' Don't be afraid of them. Remember what the Lord your God did to Pharoah and all of Egypt. You saw with your own eyes...the amazing things the Lord did. He used His mighty hand and powerful arm to bring you out. He will do the same thing to all the people you're afraid of" (Deuteronomy 7:17-19). "When you go to war against your enemies, you may see horses, chariots, and armies larger than yours. Don't be afraid of them, because the Lord your God...will be with you" (Deuteronomy 20:1).

Any leader can accomplish the task God has put before him. If it has been ordained by Him and commanded in His Word, it is the Lord's work. The question is whether leaders will continue to look at the size of the task or at the size of their God. The Lord who saved them from past "giants" can do the same in present struggles. Giants of change can be met; battles of change can be won—in His power. It is too easy to look through the wrong end of a telescope, believe a lie, and act as if God is too small! He has proven that He is able!

4. Faith-full leaders know the battle is won on their knees.

David's soul had been prepared in the fields. He had spent much time with the Lord while he was tending his father's sheep. Much of that time was spent in recalling scripture (evidenced by his vast reliance on scripture in his Psalms), prayer, and heartfelt songs of praise to the Lord.

David had gained an intimacy, a sense of oneness with his heavenly Father. God had sought for "a man after His own heart" and found him in David (1 Samuel 13:14). When the big battle came, David could rely on the God who had strengthened him over the years. His great faith gave Him the character and heart of a leader.

Leaders must prepare themselves on their knees! If they are not in a personal, daily fellowship with God, they are fighting their own battle in their own strength. God prepares leaders on their knees! That is where the greatest battle is won. If the battleground has been prepared with their faces before God, long before the battle is even in sight, leaders are conditioned to act in *faith* rather than fear. It is no different than taking an exam. Studying consistently over an entire semester gives a confidence that cannot be duplicated by an overnight "cram."

God's leaders strengthen their faith muscles with daily scripture reading and prayer. That is how God works. They let the Word dwell in them "richly" as they teach and admonish with all wisdom (Colossians 3:16). Jesus said that "Man does not live on bread alone, but on every word that comes from the mouth of God" (Matthew 4:4). There is only one way to intake the Word—to be in it daily. Leaders must personally partake of the Word in order to develop the kind of faith that produces character and heart.

5. Faith-full leaders have the proper motivation.

Fighting the battle had little to do with David himself. It was not for his own honor. It was all about God—for His glory! When David heard the awful insults Goliath was hurling toward his God, he could not stand still another moment (I Samuel 17:26, 45). He wanted to be a living testimony to the power of God. His faith would allow God to display His glory.

When God's work is done in His way, He receives glory! Now that is motivation for growing God's Church! When leaders by Christ's love bring God's people out of the cathedral-barn and into His fields, He receives glory! If a leader does the work of the church for any other reason, the leader and the church may receive recognition—but God will not be given glory. It will not be seen as a supernatural work that only God could have done. Faith enables leaders to see the greater picture in the work they are doing.

6. Faith-full leaders reject negative words from self and others.

Eliab was upset that David, his youngest brother, had even come to the battleground! "Why did you come here?" he mocked. "You came here just to see the battle" (v. 28). Saul said David was too young: "You can't fight this Philistine. You're just a boy, but he has been a warrior since he was your age" (v. 33). Goliath thought David was a joke. "Am I a dog that you come to attack me with sticks?" He called on his gods to curse David. "Come on, I'll give your body to the birds" (vv. 43-44).

Leaders can fall into the "lack of self-worth" trap. They tell themselves, "I can't." Or others tell them, "You can't." Satan says, "Are you kidding? There is no way you can do it!" If David had allowed others' words to affect his faith, he would have given up. David was nothing. He was too young. The battle was impossible. The same applies to church leaders today. They may not be experienced. They have nothing to offer in themselves.

Leaders must not allow their minds to condemn themselves. They need to take captive every thought to make it obedient to Christ (2 Corinthians 10:5)! They need to stay fixed on Jesus, to remain firm in their trust of Almighty God. Words spoken by self or others do not match up to the Word of God. Others' opinions are simply additional "giants." God chooses to use weak vessels. When weak vessels win battles, God Himself receives glory. When leaders have faith, they know the battle of change can be fought in His way—victoriously, in His strength! They demonstrate character and the heart of God!

7. Faith-full leaders believe God fully—they allow no doubt.

David believed God. He knew His promises. He had seen God work in the past and knew He would do so in the future. David declared victory before the battle was fought: "Everyone gathered here will know that the Lord can save without sword or spear, because the Lord determines every battle's outcome. He will hand all of you over to us" (v. 47).

What is faith? Corrie ten Boom defined it with the acronym "Fantastic Adventure In Trusting God." Faith is an absolute, undeniable trust in God. *He* is faith's creator and object. Victory does not rest on *faith* (having faith in *faith*). Victory rests on faith in the living *God*—the Triune God. Faith is alive! God wants to make each spiritual leader a living proof that there is a powerful, faithful God who has no limits!

Leaders who *believe* God step out and prove that God is capable of big things! When they believe God, it is a present active participle trust in *the* Lord God of the Universe! God is seeking after these types of leaders, men after His own heart. When Samuel was searching through Jesse's household for God's appointed leader, he said, "God does not see as humans see…the Lord looks into the heart" (1 Samuel 16:7). Leaders who believe God, see as He sees. These are men after His own heart.

David faced a barrier—a ten-foot barrier. But David did not flinch. Many leaders today tend to measure obstacles against their own strength. But David measured the obstacle against His *God*. He believed God. Leaders with character and God's heart make a conscious decision to keep the primary goal in front of them!

8. Faith-full leaders rely confidently on the power of God.

Saul put his battle tunic on David. He put a bronze helmet on his head and dressed him in armor. David fastened Saul's sword over his clothes and tried to walk. "I can't walk in these things," he told Saul. The weapons of the world aren't God's weapons of choice. The latest church "program" is not His method of choice.

Leaders often try to put their armor on others or put others' armor on themselves. They often lean on others' wisdom or try to pass their wisdom onto others. But for David, all it took was five smooth stones—and God said, "I'll take it from here." Faith-full leaders know that when they follow God's biblical principles, God says, "*I'll* take it from here." God had told His people, "Five of you will chase a hundred of them, and a hundred of you will chase ten thousand of them. You will defeat your enemies" (Leviticus 26:8). All God is telling His leaders now is, "No matter the odds, do it My way. I'll take it from there."

God does not want "numbers" or "methods" or "budgets" to be a factor in assessing a task. Smallness is a plus in His eyes. God is able—

He is the victor without human "weapons!" He prefers working with little. His power is sufficient. In fact, He often strips His vessels until nothing is left but their indomitable *faith* in a huge God. Then *He* is named the victor.

Faith-less leaders weary themselves by trying to succeed in their own power or in the wisdom of others. David did not fall for that error. "I come to you," he said, "in the name of the Lord" (I Samuel 17: 45). He knew he needed the supernatural. Faith-full leaders know that the indwelling presence of Jesus is always their source of strength. It is all about Him! Faith-full leaders can do all things through the strength given them by Christ (Philippians 4:13)! Their character and heart displays the strength of Christ alone!

God is God. He loves His people with a great love. He is powerful and able. Leaders with faith have God's assurance that they can complete all tasks He ordains. Leaders with His character and His heart do not see the barriers. Leaders like David see *God!* They see that the task is not their own—it is the Lord's!

DYNAMIC FACTORS FOR LEADERS

What are the dynamic factors for productive spiritual leadership? The difference is a faithful heart, one like the very heart of God. Faith-full leaders develop mature faith that has character and a heart like God. Intelligence, abilities, and skills are assumed. Good leadership principles are vital, the types of principles that can be gained from excellent books by John Maxwell and others. But it is faith that develops character and a heart like God to be productive in God's work. The mature faith of those placed in leadership is basic to growing a healthy seed-planting church.

Paul wrote to Timothy, as pastor and leader, to order certain people to stop their harmful teachings that were "off the subject." These teachings raised questions instead of promoting God's plan centered in faith. Paul's goal in giving Timothy this order was for "love to flow from a pure heart, from a clear conscious and from a sincere faith" (1 Timothy 1:3-5). He wanted Timothy to demonstrate character and a pure heart. All leaders in the church were to likewise demonstrate this heart. "Deacons must also be of good character…their wives must also be of good character" (1 Timothy 3:8, 11).

What constitutes the mature faith and good character of spiritual leaders who will guide a church to health? What defines leaders that have a heart like God's?

- They know God intimately and trust His saving and sanctifying grace (Philippians 3:8-11)
- They experience a sense of personal well-being, security and peace (Philippians 4:7,13,19)
- They integrate Christian faith and life, showing mature faith in family, work, and social relationships (James 2:14-17)
- They experience spiritual growth through Bible study and prayer (Colossians 2:6; 2 Timothy 3:14-17)
- They interact with others, building healthy relationships in their lives (1 John 1:7-8)
- They are healthy members of the Christian community of faith and support one another (Ephesians 4:12-13)
- They embrace core faith values with a personal sense of "responsibility to teach them to others" (2 Timothy 4:2)
- They celebrate the call to ministry, doing their work in joy (1 Peter 5:2)
- They actively pray for God to reveal and remove any personal baggage (1 Timothy 4:16)
- They don't let institutional bureaucracy stand in the way of ministry (2 Timothy 1:6-7; 2:14, 23-25)
- They are committed to personal development for ministry (Philippians 3:12-17)
- They lead to equip and release others to be called into various ministries (1 Peter 4:10)
- They build a leadership team by empowering and mobilizing God's people (2 Timothy 3:16-17; 4:2)
- They watch over their entrusted "flock," just as God does His (1 Peter 5:2)
- They are good examples for the believers to follow (1 Peter 5:3)
- They use God-given creative energies and instincts to overcome obstacles (2 Corinthians 1:9-11)
- They create a learning environment in their churches and are effective disciplers and mentors (2 Timothy 2:2)
- They consistently display a servant attitude (Ephesians 6:7)

Different levels of leadership require different kinds of leaders. The various levels need to be "staffed" based on the bestowal of spiritual gifts. But first and foremost, spiritual leaders must be chosen on the basis of God's criteria—from scripture. They need to demonstrate a mature faith—strong character and a heart like God's. Those are what make the difference!

Pastors and spiritual leaders are to be productive partakers of the divine power for everything they need for life and for godliness. Peter emphasizes the importance of a mature faith, heart, and character. "God's divine power has given us everything we need for life and for godliness," he says. "This power was given to us through knowledge of the one who called us by His own glory and integrity. Through His glory and integrity He has given us His promises that are of the highest value. Through these promises you will share in the divine nature because you have escaped the corruption that sinful desires cause in the world." (2 Peter 1: 3-4)

"Because of this, make every effort to add integrity to your faith; and to integrity add knowledge; to knowledge add self-control; to self-control add endurance; to endurance add godliness; to godliness add Christian affection; and to Christian affection add love. If you have these qualities and they are increasing, it demonstrates that your knowledge about our Lord Jesus Christ is living and productive. If these qualities aren't present in your life, you're shortsighted and have forgotten that you were cleansed from your past sins" (2 Peter 1:5-9). Such are the qualities of a seed-planting, nurturing leader.

Church leaders are not leaders because they were elected to a leadership position. They are leaders because God called them, because God gives them the faith, character and heart to lead.

CHAPTER 9

If You Want Spiritual Fruit, You Have to Get Out of the Cathedral-Barn

John Ortberg's *If You Want to Walk on Water, You've Got to Get Out of the Boat*[1] challenges spiritual leaders to take the big step of faith. He invites them to walk where Jesus calls. While fear of inadequacy may visit their lives and ministries, they still experience God's powerful presence and promise. As they discern God's call, they will choose to go beyond their fears, get out of the cathedral-barn, and walk by faith into God's field.

In fear, eleven disciples remained in the boat. By faith, Peter walked on the water. He walked toward Jesus, "but when he noticed how strong the wind was, he became afraid and started to sink. He shouted, 'Lord, save me!' Jesus reached out, caught hold of him and said, 'You have so little faith! Why did you doubt?'" (Matthew 14:30-31). The fact is, if anyone wants to walk on water, they must get out of the boat—despite doubts.

Winds and storms are no surprise. Neither are hesitating, faltering leaders—nor dull, weak members. The question is whether spiritual leaders will reach out to Jesus in faith. Will they ask the Holy Spirit for strength to get out of the cathedral-barn? At times they may walk into stiff winds of opposition. But do they recognize that these winds blow them onto paths leading directly to members in great spiritual need? Will they focus on the storm or on Jesus—on the problem or on the Word?

There is more to life than sitting in a boat. There is more to Christ's mission than sitting in church worship services or meetings. Jesus wants leaders to be leading their people into God's field, not merely meet in the cathedral-barn. In God's field they will find acres of plants to tend, where they will experience His abundant growth and blessing.

THE BUSINESS OF THE CHURCH IS *GROWING*

A nursery sells plants and trees by telling the public, "Our business is *growing*." Its future depends on growing healthy plants and trees. The biblical church can also claim, "Our business is *growing*." This is God's directive for the Church!

- John 11:15—Jesus wants His disciples to *grow* in faith.
- Acts 20:32—The Word makes God's people *grow*.
- 1 Corinthians 14:3—Speaking God's Word helps people *grow*.
- 1 Corinthians 14:4-5, 12—Speaking God's Word helps the church *grow*.
- 2 Peter 3:18—God wants His people to *grow* in the knowledge of Jesus.
- Philippians 1:9—Love will *grow* because of knowledge and insight.

Indeed, both nurseries and churches are in the growth business. Forces of growth are positive! Growth changes the scenery. It changes the yield. The decision to view growth—and change—as a positive force in ministry unleashes needed energy! Explosive energy! Seed-planting churches thrive on this kind of energy.

The sculpture of a sower stands on the dome of the Nebraska State Capitol building. This image demonstrates the most basic principle for seed-planting and growth. Before there is any hope for the harvest, the seed must be planted and nurtured. What farm would advertise, "Our business is harvesting?" What corporation would advertise, "Our business is marketing?" The business of the church is not harvesting! Harvesting is Jesus' task. *He* is the One who calls workers into the harvest when the fruit is ripe.

The hymn, "Fruitful Trees, the Spirit's Sowing,"[2] aptly expresses the Spirit's role in the growth business of the Church:

Fruitful trees, the Spirit's sowing, May we ripen and increase;
Fruit to life eternal growing, Rich in love and joy and peace.

Laden branches freely bearing, Gifts the Giver loves to bless;
Here is fruit that grows by sharing, Patience, kindness, gentleness.

Rooted deep in Christ our Master, Christ our pattern and our goal;
Teach us as the years fly faster, Goodness, faith and self-control.

Fruitful trees, the Spirit's tending, May we grow till harvests cease;
Till we taste, in life unending, Heaven's love and joy and peace.

Seeds do not grow in the bin. Members do not grow when the cathedral-barn is in a maintenance or survival mode. Harvesting churches have wandered far too long in the wilderness of programs and institutionalism. After forty years of wilderness life, God told Israel it had stayed at Mount Horeb long enough. He said, "Break camp, and get ready!" (Deuteronomy 1:6-7). He told them to enter and take possession of the land that He had promised them. Moses said, "The Lord your God is giving you this land. Go ahead! Take possession of it…Don't be afraid or terrified" (1:21). Likewise, it's time for pastors and spiritual leaders to announce to their congregations that they are leaving the mountain of maintenance and harvesting. They are entering the land of seed-planting and nurturing!

Isaiah foretold of John the Baptizer, the voice crying out in the desert to God's people, Israel. These words echo a fitting message for harvesting churches. Are they ready to get out of the institutional wilderness and off of the mountain of fear? "Clear a way for the Lord. Make a straight highway in the wilderness for our God. Every valley will be raised. Every mountain and hill will be lowered. Steep places will be made level. Rough places will be smooth. Then the Lord's glory will be revealed and all people will see it together" (Isaiah 40:3-5).

God sends His servants into the promised land of seed-planting, nurturing, and mission. He does so, not with a word of law, but with the word of gospel and forgiveness. God's message is the same as His word to His errant people Israel: "Comfort my people! Comfort them!" says your God, "Speak tenderly to Jerusalem and announce to it that its time of hard labor is over and its wrongs have been paid for" (Isaiah 40:1).

God's message on the mountain changed from fear to faith. "Go up a high mountain, Zion. Tell the good news! Call out with a loud voice…raise your voice without fear" (Isaiah 40:9). The same message is spoken by the voices of pastors and spiritual leaders who choose to guide their people to become seed-planting, nurturing communities of faith.

God's people in the Old Testament were required to follow His guidance in order to leave the mountain of fear and enter the promised land of seed-planting and harvest. Those who commit themselves to building seed-planting, nurturing churches must hear the Word of the Lord. The message Moses shared with Israel applies to God's people today. "Israel, what does the Lord your God want you to do? He wants you to fear Him, follow all His directions, love Him, and worship Him with all your heart and with all your soul. The Lord wants you to obey His commands and laws that I am giving you today for your own good" (Deuteronomy 10:12-13).

God had reminded Israel that He was giving it the promised land, everything it needed for abundant living. "The Lord set his heart on you and chose you…you were chosen because the Lord loved you" (Deuteronomy 7:7-8). Israel was chosen to be His beloved, to represent Him and to do His work. So, seed-planting congregations will heed God's call, "Love the Lord your God, and do what He wants you to do" (Deuteronomy 11:1). Is there any question that God wants His people to follow His agenda, to pursue His goals?

Every decision in Israel's walk with God counted. Each choice made was an indication of its faith in God—or residual doubt, the decision to trust in its own wisdom. Every step it took, no matter whether taken in faith or in doubt, mattered. Israel needed to leave its weaknesses and fear behind. For a moment in its history, Israel did exactly that. At the Jordan River, Israel trusted the word of God and went forward boldly. It believed God, did what He said, left fear behind, and "got out of the boat."

The congregation taking steps into seed-planting, nurturing fields must do the same. Seed-planting leaders will no longer struggle to function in stale traditional maintenance modes or to depend on a bureaucracy of complex rules and guidelines. They will not depend on programs entrenched in traditions which stifle creativity. Rather, they will choose to create paths and roads that will reach all people in God's field. Living faith is the fuel that will hold them up and keep them focused on Jesus. They know that, whenever Jesus calls someone out of the cathedral-barn, He gives power to go out to the fields. They go out to reach people. Living faith is patient, disciplined, confident, waiting for God to guide. Leaders must actively trust God in their discussion, planning, and strategizing. They must walk—perhaps slowly at first, but ever determined—gaining momentum as they nurture the field.

Scripture is filled with promises for those who wait on the Lord. The directive is clear: "Go in God's strength, wisdom, and guidance! Let God's Word personally speak to you! As you lead and walk by faith, Christ is in you!" There is no greater reality for church leaders. These are all the resources needed. It is all about Him!

It does not take genius leadership to form and facilitate a seed-planting community of faith. The Holy Spirit has already bestowed required gifts of leadership upon exactly those whom He has chosen to use. A new sense of story is needed—the gospel narrative—that instructs the ministry of the congregation. The church is a nurturing, mission community with the saving gospel of Jesus Christ! It exists, locally and worldwide, to make disciples. The gospel message is not merely one of gaining. The mission is to live in Christian community here on earth, in a way that extends to eternity.

The seeds grow! The Word works! "Listen! A farmer went to plant seed" (Mark 4:3). Jesus said, "the kingdom of God is like a man who scatters seeds on the ground" (Mark 4:26). Jesus asked, "How can we show what the kingdom of God is like? To what can we compare it? It's like a mustard seed planted in the ground" (Mark 4:30-31). "The farmer plants the Word" (Mark 4:14). Be a seed-planter! Be a seed-planting church!

So, don't put your dreams away for another day! Walk where Jesus calls. Be a seed-planter that changes lives! Be a spiritual leader that no longer hangs around the cathedral-barn, but hangs around hurting persons in God's field. Be an outward-focused church that demonstrates love for God's people. Be a visionary church that risks itself and its resources to nurture every member. Be an effective church that pursues its goal with prayer and passion. Be a church determined to fully explore its vision. Be a Christ-focused church determined to display the glory of God!

APPENDIX A

PERSONAL DISCIPLESHIP INVENTORY

What does it mean to be a disciple? Together, the seven areas listed below profile a "fully-devoted follower of Jesus." Based on biblical references, these areas represent the work of over 100 members of Gloria Dei studying the life of a disciple. This inventory allows you to measure your progress, at this time, as a fully devoted follower of Jesus.

This is **your** personal tool for assessment. Your answers will not be shared with anyone. These questions are not meant to be invasive or threatening, but are meant to help you know where you stand as you look forward to becoming mature, attaining to the whole measure of the fullness of Christ (Eph. 4:13).

Self-reflection can be a difficult process, but the more honest and objective your answers are, the more useful this tool will be for you. Taking this inventory each year may help you measure your lifelong growth as you walk alongside Jesus. Your answers will help you to focus on important areas for growth and celebration.

Please circle the best answer for both Yes/No and numerical responses. (5= Always/Completely; 4= Mostly/Often; 3= Somewhat/Occasionally; 2= Not Much/Rarely; 1= Not at all/Never. Use additional paper to answer the open-ended questions in detail. Pray that God uses this tool to provide you with important feedback as you follow your Personal Discipleship Plan.

Public Commitment: Fully devoted followers of Jesus are active participants in a local Christian congregation, worshipping and communing on a regular basis. (Psalm 122:1; Heb. 10:25; Acts 2:42)

1. I have been baptized. ___Yes ___No
2. I attend worship weekly. ___Yes ___No

3. If not, how often do I attend worship per month? 1 2 3

4. I am a member of Gloria Dei Lutheran Church. ___Yes ___No

5. I participate in communion (the Lord's Supper) as often as it is available. ___Yes ___No

6. I am currently involved in some sort of service activity (non-worship) through Gloria Dei. ___Yes ___No

7. I believe that baptism is a sacrament and the work of the Holy Spirit to bring about faith. ___Yes ___No

8. I believe that communion is a sacrament and a work of the Holy Spirit to sustain faith. ___Yes ___No

Lifestyle: Fully devoted followers of Jesus mature in their faith, daily demonstrating true Christian character in both speech and behavior. They continue to replace bad (unhealthy) habits with good (healthy) ones. They give God first priority in life, living in a state of trust, hope, and anticipation to His glory (John 15:8; Prov. 9:9-10; Col. 2:6; Acts 17:11; Acts 2:47; Romans 12:2; Tim. 3:14-17). Rate each of the following 1 to 5:

1. I daily read and study God's Word.

2. I feel that I am growing in my knowledge and understanding of God's Word.

3. I evaluate all teaching, ideas, values and lifestyles to see if they are consistent with the Bible.

4. Worship, praising, and thanking God throughout the day is part of my lifestyle.

5. I truly look forward to, enjoy, and am transformed by attending worship with other Christians.

6. My daily choices and decisions are based on Biblical principles and values.

7. I follow (obey) the guidance of the Holy Spirit.

8. I am actively breaking unhealthy habits that cause me distraction in my journey as a fully devoted follower.

9. I am living in a state of hope and trust, because of God's love and forgiveness.

10. I participate in a small group Bible study that meets at least twice each month.

11. I am perceived by others as being trustworthy.
12. I have come to a point where I believe God has forgiven me for all I've done.
13. I forgive persons for what they have done for me, fully and freely.
14. I exhibit a good relationship with my spouse/family.
15. I experience full belief in God as He works supernaturally in my life.
A. Which parts of my lifestyle are pleasing to God?
B. Which parts of my lifestyle are not pleasing to God and how do I plan to change them?
C. What addictive, recurring sins (or memories) are inhibiting my growth as a fully devoted follower?

Witness: Fully devoted followers of Jesus delight in their roles as witnesses to the good news of Jesus. They pray for non-Christians, boldly seizing opportunities for interaction and contagiously sharing the love of Jesus with them. They are authentic and winsome in their witness, displaying God-given strength and stability in all they do (1 Pet. 3:15-16; Col. 4:3-6; Mark 5:19-20; Acts 5:42; Acts 22:14-15; 1 Thes. 2:4). Rate each of the following 1 to 5:

1. I effectively share my faith in Jesus Christ with non-Christians.
2. I intentionally develop and maintain relationships with non-Christians with the hope of someday sharing Jesus with them.
3. I have memorized specific Scriptures in order to present the Gospel to others.
4. I am able to clearly explain what I believe and why.
5. I see that the people who have responded to my witness receive the spiritual follow-up and continual support they need.
6. I regularly pray for the salvation of specific non-Christians I know.
A. When people ask me about my faith, how do I normally respond?
B. What is hindering me from being a more effective witness?
C. What must I do to become a more effective witness of the gospel?

Prayer: Fully devoted followers of Jesus develop a disciplined prayer life, complete with meditation, study, and fasting. They experience the power of prayer and believe that for God, nothing is impossible (Luke 11:1-4; Acts 5:12-16; Acts 13:1-3; Acts 14:23; 2 Tim. 3:14-17). Rate each of the following 1 to 5:

1. I pray daily.
2. I have a prayer plan or method, as well as a time set aside for prayer in my life.
3. I respectfully enter God's presence with awe, humility, gratitude, and expectancy.
4. I find myself praying constantly, both speaking to God and listening to Him.
5. My prayer life is effective and rewarding.
6. I regularly see God's intervention in the lives of those for whom I am praying.
7. I take time to be perfectly still before the Lord by meditating on Him or a passage in His Word
8. I take prayer issues before the Lord within the discipline of fasting.
A. Regarding prayer, what developments would I like to see both in me and in my prayer life?

Care: Fully devoted followers of Jesus are open and sensitive to the needs, successes, and problems of others. They join or form a group for support and accountability and are able to keep confidences. They are willing to be mentored and mentor others (Acts 2:44,45; Eph. 4:32). Rate the following from 1 to 5:

1. I show love to others.
2. I build relationships with people I serve.
3. I allow people in my congregation to love and serve me.
4. Other people hold me accountable for my growth as a fully-devoted follower.
5. I invest time in relationships with other congregation members outside of the "church" context.
6. I commit to serving people who do not belong to my congregation as well as those who do.

APPENDIX A

7. I desire to learn how to share my faith with people with whom I have a relationship.

A. What can I do to make a difference in the lives of others?

B. In what ways do I demonstrate God's unconditional love in my familial relationships?

Spiritual Gifts: Fully devoted followers of Jesus identify and use unique abilities to the glory of God and His Church. They learn and develop skills that prepare them to serve, encouraging and supporting others to do the same (Rom. 12:6-8; 1 Cor. 12:4-11; Eph. 4:11-13; 1 Pet. 4:10-11). Rate the following from 1 to 5:

1. I have identified my spiritual gifts within the past five years.

2. I make use of my spiritual gifts by regularly using them to serve God and His people.

3. Others have confirmed my spiritual gifts.

A. What ministry areas are of interest to me? Do these fit with my identified spiritual gifts?

B. With what ministry can I be involved to enhance the use of my spiritual giftedness?

Finance and Stewardship: Fully devoted followers of Jesus realize that God graciously promises to provide all that is needed, including money (Luke 11:11-13; Mal. 3:10). They are therefore not preoccupied or obsessed with the accumulation of income of possessions (Heb. 13:5). They are comfortable talking about money and understand that the church has a God-given responsibility to talk about it (1 Tim. 6:6-10). Rate the following 1 to 5:

1. I give at least 10% of my gross income to the Lord's work (2 Cor. 9:6-8).

2. I joyfully share with those in need (Matt. 19:21).

3. I am effectively managing all that God has given to me (family, time, talents, intellect, relationships, possessions, etc.).

4. I donate my skills to my congregation and to further God's kingdom.

5. I make money ethically and pay taxes honestly (Rom. 13:7).
6. I spend money wisely, pay bills on time, and avoid destructive debt (Rom. 13:8).
7. I save consistently.
A. What does the concept of stewardship mean to me?
B. To what extent do I feel that I sacrifice my resources to facilitate impact for Christ?

Summary: This is not a "test" to compare yourself against another person or norming pool. However, the relative scores of your responses, combined with your reflective comments to the open-ended questions could suggest areas for which you may want to establish discipleship goals. Use the table below to summarize your assessment and begin the discipleship planning process. May you see God's blessings in this effort!

"Let the peace of Christ rule in your hears, since as members of one body you were called to peace. And be thankful. Let the word of Christ dwell in you richly as you teach and admonish one another with all wisdom, and as you sing psalms, hymns and spiritual songs with gratitude in your hearts to God. And whatever you do, whether in word or deed, do it all in the name of the Lord Jesus, giving thanks to God the Father through him." (Colossians 3:15-17)

CHARACTERISTIC	SCORE/ # OF YES RESPONSES	POTENTIAL AREAS FOR IMPROVEMENT (E.G. "PRAYING FOR FAMILY," "NOT IN SMALL GROUP," "IRREGULAR WORSHIP ATTENDANCE," "HAVE NEVER FASTED BEFORE")
Public Commitment		
Lifestyle		
Witness		
Prayer		
Care		
Spiritual Gifts		
Finances and Stewardship		

Becoming a fully devoted follower of Jesus is a life long pursuit. We have individually experienced our discipleship journey a little differently. We have different paces and different life experiences that add texture and richness to our lives in Christ.

APPENDIX A

A disciple's spiritual life may look like a line graph:

- Ups and downs of possible growth, with the ups not necessarily being "happy times" in the disciple's life, but are times when the Lord's work was clearly evident
- Ups and downs may look less and less like an EKG readout as one matures and is prepared for greater challenges.
- Times of preparation for challenges ahead may look like "plateaus," yet they are important for our spiritual development

The depth of the sharing is entirely up to the DISCIPLE as discipleship is very personal.

QUESTIONS TO CONSIDER AS YOU PREPARE YOUR PERSONAL DISCIPLESHIP PLAN

1. Which area(s) seem to need the most improvement, support, or strengthening?
2. What activities currently offered at Gloria Dei could assist with these needs?
3. Do any of your responses suggest that you may need help from a counselor or Stephen Minister?

As a member of the Christian church and in response to the grace of God poured out for me in the death and resurrection of Jesus, I plan to devote myself to the discipline of following Jesus. I realize that I will never obtain "the full measure of the fullness of Christ" before I join Him in heaven, yet I know that God's blessings in this life will be made even more clear to me as I follow Jesus daily. I am forgiven. I am loved by the Creator of the universe. The Holy Spirit is working in my life giving me the strength and guidance I need to fulfill God's plan for my life. To God be the glory.

Disciple's Signature   Date

I will pray for, encourage, and support this disciple to the best of my ability through the power of the Holy Spirit. I will hold this plan in confidence and protect this relationship.

Assistant Lay Minister's Signature   Date

Note: The "Personal Discipleship Inventory" was created and used by Gloria Dei Lutheran Church, 18220 Upper Bay Road, Houston, TX 77058-4198 *gloriadei@gdlc.org*. It is still in the process of development. Used by permission.

ENDNOTES

INTRODUCTION

[1] "The Third Coming of George Barna," *Christianity Today*, August 2002, p. 33-38.

[2] Ibid. Condensed by Stafford from Barna's "The State of the Church 2002" Issachar.

CHAPTER 3

[1] Christian Schwarz, **Natural Church Development** (ChurchSmart Resources, 3830 Ohio Avenue, St. Charles, IL 60174-5462, 1996, ISBN 1-889638-00-S).

[2] Ibid. p. 10.

[3] Ibid. p. 12.

[4] Ibid. p. 14.

[5] Ibid. p. 89.

[6] Ibid. p. 89.

[7] Ibid. p. 76.

[8] M. Robert Mulholland, Jr., **Shaped by the Word** (Nashville: The Upper Room, 1985, pgs. 129-132)

[9] Ibid., pages 27-29.

[10] Ibid., p. 110.

[11] Barna, G., *Ministry Currents*, October-December, 1961, pg. 9.

[12] Schultz, Tom and Joani, WHY NOBODY LEARNS MUCH OF ANYTHING AT CHURCH: And How To Fix It. Loveland, CO: Group, 1996, pg. 10.

[13] Smith, F. *Insult to Intelligence*. Portsmotuh, NH: Heinemann, 1988, pg. 80.

CHAPTER 4

[1]Grasp. *Mountain Movers International*, 4000 Midway Road, Suite 303, Carrollton, TX 75007 214-435-0753 Whamit@aol.com Website: Mountainmovers.org

CHAPTER 5

[1]NEIBAUER PRESS, 20 Industrial Drive, Warminster, PA 18974-1465, 1-800-322-6203 e-mail Nathan@Neibauer.com; fax: 215-322-2495; website: www.churchstewardship.com. An Appendix to this book provides full information regarding all the resources on stewardship of giving available from NEIBAUER PRESS.

The four messages and studies in *New Beginnings...In Christian Living and Giving* are 1) Changing from Institutional to Biblical Christian; 2) Trust and Obey Only God; 3) Do What God Wants You to Do; 4) Lord, Touch Our Eyes Again so that We may See Clearly.

The eight messages and studies in *Big Step Forward in Faith* are: 1) Born to Serve Our Creator; 2) Civil War: the New Man's Victory Over the Old Man; 3) Seek God First; 4) Live Worthy of Our Call to Serve God; 5) You Have a Story to Tell; 6) The First and Big Stewardship Offering; Our Repentant heart; 7) God's Rich Supply for Our Faithful Giving; 8) The Grace-based, Word-grounded, Gospel-driven, Spirit-powered, Mission-directed, Book of Acts Church. The book offers six responsive prayers with stewardship and mission emphases.

Lord, Let It Happen To Me As You Said has six sermons and Bible studies, plus a booklet, with the following topics: 1) Faithful Christian stewards experience the victory of the New Self over the Old Self; 2) The first stewardship offering is the repentant heart; 3) We are created in Christ for doing good works; 4) Avoid giving leftovers to God; 5) Give to God first; 6) Trust God's promises.

I Am Ready To Live offers messages and studies, together with a booklet, on the following topics: 1) Having Christ as the Center and right Christian goals; 2) Real security, happiness and success comes from trusting and obeying Christ; 3) Jesus wants us to have the abundant life; 4) Productive and successful living begins with God's goodness; 5) Fruitful living involves faithful use of abilities and spiritual gifts; 6) Enlarge your life's influence by investing firstfruits for God's work.

The Nurturing Church Generates Grace Giving, Waldo Werning (Neibauer Press, 2003). This is a fresh and unique, one-of-a-kind book to help a church to transition in stewardship and giving from a traditional, maintenance, harvesting church to a seed-planting, nurturing, mission church. It presents a grace stewardship system which is an "energy field" flowing from the explosive Word to grow productive stewards. Rev. Larry Reinhardt, Director of LCMS Stewardship Ministry calls it a "no-nonsense approach to grace-based preaching and teaching of real biblical stewardship. Principles and lessons are wonderfully biblical, clear practical and workable with encouragement to avoid appeals based on budgets and needs. There is a wealth of food for thought and actions." It shows how abundant planting and nurturing produces abundant stewardship harvests. ChurchSmart Publishers have graciously permitted the publishing of Chapter 5 as the book, *The Nurturing Church Generates Grace Giving*, available from Neibauer Press.

[2]Crown Financial Ministries, 601 Broad Street SE, Gainesville, GA 30501 (1-800-722-1976) website: crown.org

[3]New Beginnings and Big Step forward in Faith

[4]Booklets available from Neibauer Press.

CHAPTER 6

[1]Gleaned from an article, "Plantin' and Pickin'," by John Ian Adnams, The Canadian Lutheran, Sept. 2002, pg. 5.

[2]Waldo J. Werning, **Spiritual Travel Guide**, available from the Website www.healthychurch.com.

[3]Document which lists E.B. Hill as the author, but without indicating the source.

[4]Judson Cornwall, *Let Us Enjoy Forgiveness* (Old Tappan, NJ, Fleming H. Rebell, 1978), pg. 72.

[5]Ibid., Page 159.

CHAPTER 7

[1]Christian Schwarz, **Natural Church Development** page 40.

[2]Waldo J. Werning, **12 Pillars of a Healthy Church** (ChurchSmart Resources, 3830 Ohio Avenue, St. Charles, IL 60174-5462, 2001).

[3]Rick Warren, **The Purpose Driven Church** (Zondervan Publishing House, Grand Rapids, Michigan 49530, 1995).

[4] Schwarz, Ibid, page 38.

[5] Ibid, page 39.

[6] Ibid, page 40.

[7] The Survey is available from ChurchSmart Resources, 3830 Ohio Ave., St. Charles, IL 60174-5462, tel. 1-800-253-4276.

[8] Waldo J. Werning, **12 PILLARS of a Healthy Church** (St. Charles, IL, ChurchSmart, 2001).

[9] *The Health Church-Sermons and Bible Studies*, Development Department, Concordia University, 2811 NE Holman Street, Portland, OR 97211 (ph) 503-288-9371.

[10] Rick Warren, **The Purpose-Driven™ Church** (Grand Rapids: Zondervan Publishing House, 1995)

[11] Illustration taken from **The Purpose-Driven™ Church** by Rick Warren, Copyright 1995 by Rick Warren. Used by permission of Zondervan Publishing House.

[12] This "Personal Discipleship Inventory" was created and is used by Gloria Dei Lutheran Church, 18220 Upper Bay Road, Houston, TX, 77058-4198, ph (281) 333-4535, fax (281)335-0574, gloriadei@gdlc.org. Used by permission.

CHAPTER 8

[1] Adams, Scott. *Dilbert* (2002 United Feature Syndicate, Inc).

[2] I am grateful to my daughter, Sharon Jones (MSM, MBS), for providing the Bible study about David.

CHAPTER 9

[1] John Ortberg, *If You Want to Walk on Water, You've Got to Get Out of the Boat* (Grand Rapids, MI: Zondervan Publishing House, 2001)

[2] Music by Ralph C. Schulz, Text by Timothy Dudley Smith, Hope Publishing Company. Hymnal Supplement 1998. H59, Concordia Publishing House.

COMMENDATIONS FOR THE SEED-PLANTING BOOK

The Church Doctor, Kent R. Hunter, Corunna, IN: "I enjoyed reading this! It is outstanding, with Biblical depth, powerfully practical. This strong and useful work by Waldo Werning will change you and your church from maintenance to mission, from harvest to seed planting and nurturing, and from a bureaucracy to the movement that God has called Christianity to be. If everyone in a local church would read, study and apply these Biblical truths, it would transform each of those people and the church to be what God intended it to be. For those who area tired of playing church in the world of ecclesiastical dissfunctionality, this is the seed material that can bring new life to your congregation. I have already begun using this material in my work with churches."

Dr. Elmer L. Towns, Dean, School of Religion, Liberty University, Lynchburg, VA "Werning has seen a neglected niche in church planting and has written a well-crafted book to meet that need. The Seed-Planting Church is what each church should do for us who believe in "harvest theology." The problem is, too many modern churches are tied to a program, or maintenance. Just as every person who plants a seed looks forward to the harvest, so the local church is a seed that should bring forth the harvest in growing churches, new saints in the kingdom, an new churches that continue the process of planting other churches."

Dr. Robert J. Scudieri, Director for North America, LCMS World Mission: "Waldo Werning has put his finger on the basic issue of the church in North America. Will it be an institution or will it be part of the missional movement? The great majority of our churches are organized around programs. How much more powerful would they be? How much more vital would the witness be, if they were organized around God's Word and His Sacraments, which impel to mission? Werning's point of view is one that is surely needed today."

Dr. Gary L. McIntosh, Professor, Christian Ministry and Leadership, Talbot School of Theology: "Every once in awhile, a new book comes along and challenges us to think 'outside the box.' Such is The Seed-Planting Church. Reading it will challenge you to become a more faithful coworker—God's farmer—by planting and nurturing God's Word in the hearts of receptive people. The business of the church is growing. Growth—spiritual and numerically—is God's directive for the Church. Yet, as most of us reluctantly admit, not many local congregations are faithful to God's design.

The Seed-Planting Church declares that the key issue is not one of failed leadership; rather it is a failure to have the correct design. The author, Waldo Werning, proposes a radical, redesign of church strategy based on Biblical principles and examples. Looking at the church as an 'agricultural project,' this book is a welcome addition to the field of church growth and health."

Dr. Ken Behnken, Center for U.S. Missions, Concordia University, Irvine, CA "A trip to a modern day Iowa farm and a review of the Biblical agriculture narratives provide Waldo Werning, the author, with a powerful metaphor to help us distinguish the problems facing today's churches. He contrasts the harvesting church caught up in programs, and man made growth stimulants to increase numbers with the nurturing church focused on, planting the seed, nurturing the plants with the Word of God to increase the number of disciples, leaving the growth to God. He concludes with a great summary of the books focus, 'A spiritual leader no longer hangs around the cathedral-barn, but hangs around hurting persons in God's field.' The church is not about buildings and programs—it is about people and disciples. The author helps us refocus on the Biblical concept of the church as the living body of Jesus Christ. An excellent book to help us get our priorities back in line with Biblical perspective as we are privileged to serve in the fields of His Kingdom."

COMMENDATIONS

Dr. Paul Anderson, Director of Lutheran Renewal, President of the Master Institute: "Most of the church is stuck in a programatic methodology with regard to church health and growth. Dr. Werning's book offers a Biblically based, spirit-empowered, and grace-oriented option for the church—the seed-planting, nurturing church. Such a reorientation for those 80% that are into maintenance more than mission will move them from expediency to efficiency and effectiveness. Way to go, Waldo!"

Dr. Dann Spader, SonLife, Elburn, IL: "Dr. Werning has captured some very helpful insights in Scriptural agrarian concepts. The Bible uses more farming terminology than CEO terminology—a helpful distinctive to those seeking to nurture church health. With his years of experience, you will find Dr. Werning's insights helpful—perhaps even life-changing as you 'renew your mind' towards a nurturing style of leadership."

Hugh Townsend, North American Mission Board, Southern Baptist Convention: "Dr. Werning provides an excellent resource for Pastors and lay leaders who are tired of toiling in fruitlessness and want to see their church come alive with hope and produce many new disciples of Christ. The book challenges the myth that leadership is the problem for so many struggling churches today. Dr. Werning maintains the issue that the church has the wrong design. Using what he refers to as the organic or agricultural approach, he leads the church from a maintenance or programmatic approach to become a missional, seed-planting one. The approach provides a strong biblical basis of both principles and examples. The author challenges churches and their leaders to free themselves from man-made constraints and return to God ordained principles of seed-planting and nurturing."